D1168422

Drinking with Miss Dutchie

DRINKING WITH

MISS DUTCHIE

a memoir

ED BRESLIN

Thomas Dunne Books

St. Martin's Press 🐾 New York

THOMAS DUNNE BOOKS.

An imprint of St. Martin's Press.

DRINKING WITH MISS DUTCHIE. Copyright © 2011 by Ed Breslin. All rights
reserved. Printed in the United States of America. For information, address
St. Martin's Press, 175 Fifth Avenue, New York, N.Y. 10010.

Excerpt from "To Make Them Monumental" from *Speech, for Instance* by
Sidney Goldfarb. Reprinted by permission of Farrar, Straus and Giroux,
LLC. Copyright © 1969 by Sidney Goldfarb.

Excerpt from *A Life in Letters* by Matthew Bruccoli, editor. Reprinted
with the permission of Scribner, a Division of Simon & Schuster. Inc.
Copyright © 1994 by The Trustees under agreement dated July 3, 1975,
created by Frances Scott Fitzgerald Smith. All rights reserved.

www.thomasdunnebooks.com

www.stmartins.com

Book design by Michelle McMillian

Library of Congress Cataloging-in-Publication Data

Breslin, Ed.

Drinking with Miss Dutchie : a memoir / Ed Breslin. — 1st ed.

p. cm.

ISBN 978-0-312-61975-6 (alk. paper)

1. Breslin, Ed. 2. Publishers and publishing—United States—
Biography. 3. Human–animal relationships. 4. Editors—United
States—Biography. 5. Book editors—United States—Biography.
6. Dogs. I. Title.

Z473.B796A3 2011

070.5092—dc22

[B]   2010039302

First Edition: March 2011

10 9 8 7 6 5 4 3 2 1

This book is for Lynn Dreese Breslin

and

in memory of Margaret Marie Kelly Breslin,

James Bernard Breslin, William F. Kelly,

Thomas A. Leonard, Mary Ellen Leonard Weinberg,

and

in celebration of Mary Theresa Kelly Leonard

Acknowledgments

At St. Martin's, for outstanding support, enthusiasm, and all-around book publishing excellence, I thank my gracious publisher, Tom Dunne, his assistant, the affable Margaret Smith, my extraordinary editor Marcia Markland, her right hand, assistant editor Kat Brzozowski, my nimble publicists, the effervescent John Murphy and John Karle, and the gifted art director Michael Storrings, who designed this book's cover. Copy editor Fran Fisher did an excellent job, which I much appreciate, as did book designer Michelle McMillian and production editor Kenneth J. Silver, both of whose mastery of the art of bookmaking speaks for itself.

I extend a warm thanks to my great friend and unwavering supporter Sally Richardson, president of St. Martin's, and to her nonpareil assistant and colleague, Chris Holder. Their aura together is as inspiring as that famous tide that lifts all boats.

My early readers deserve a special salute: Gene Labocetta, who first told me I had something here; Geoff Hannell, my steady and unstinting coach; George Williamson, who bristles with wisdom and energy; the keen-eyed and incisive Jamie Raab; the perspicacious Jonathan Segal; Keith Hollaman, whose insight and judgment never lapse; Paul Oppenheimer, whose few words had a large impact; those sagacious editorial legends, Hugh Van Dusen and the late Larry Ashmead; and Michael Goedhuis, whose intuition and discernment never flag.

The following, all friends I cherish, warrant a big thanks: Marty Asher, Eddie Bell, Jerry Bernhardt, Bob Bohan, Julia Cameron, Ed Carpenter, Bill Chivil, Frank Curtis, Warren Gold, Larry Grobel, Leigh Haber, Alex Hoyt, Christine Hughes, Howard Kaminsky, Jessica Kovar, Jonathon Lazear, Tommy Leonard, Jack Lichtenstein, Joe Mastrangelo, Dan McNally, Gene Mydlowski, Jerry Orter, Molly O'Neill, Frank Pellegrino, Vince Pomilio, Todd Reinglass, Ahouva Rubenstein, Howard Taggart, and Agostino von Hassell.

Bill Strachan and Sean Desmond, distinguished publishers, as well as talented agents Elaine Markson and Esther Newberg, each gave me a big boost when I needed it, as did renowned publicist Lynn Goldberg.

The doctors and staff of the New Baltimore Animal

Hospital were never less than kind and helpful, for which I am most grateful.

Indiana University librarians Nels Gunderson and Angela Kilsdonk patiently answered my questions and provided much needed details.

Many thanks to those two great dog lovers: Shelly Hébert and Karen Smith, and to equestrian and horse lover extraordinaire Amanda Baird.

PART ONE

And how shall I deck my song
for the large sweet soul that has gone?

—WALT WHITMAN,
"When Lilacs Last in the Dooryard Bloomed"

CHAPTER ONE

Her front legs were too short. I would never have known this and cared less, but a breeder with knowledge of Labrador retrievers pointed it out to me after I told him of comments Miss Dutchie had drawn on walks with me in New York City. Calling her Miss Dutchie with the formal Southern twist was my idea; I added it to amuse myself and because she always seemed to have an extra-regal feminine presence about her that wasn't done justice by simply calling her Dutchie. My wife had formally named her Pennsylvania Dutchess, and that's what we entered on the forms for the Kennel Club of America. The forms were given to me by the breeder I bought her from and I figured I might as well follow through and fill them out, even though we had no intentions of breeding her. Though every day that passes I wish I had bred her if I could have one of her puppies to comfort me now.

Miss Dutchie was euthanized five weeks ago. It was the most painful thing I've ever gone through. I had no idea losing a pet could be so painful. I had been through the wrenching loss of a parent, but I had not lived with that parent, my father, for the thirty-eight years prior to his death.

Her loss I cannot get used to. Her absence is the greatest presence in my life. It presses against my consciousness every hour of every day, sometimes every minute of every hour, for long stretches. This is not a slight to my wife, whom I adore. In fact, Lynn and I are in the same painful funk, a nearly paralyzing cafard. Neither of us can adjust to Dutchie's loss. We carry on, we do what we have to do, but emotionally we don't move on. We are both learning in a profound way, me I suspect more than Lynn, what Dutchie meant to us on a permanent basis. For an hour tonight here in the country we sat on the sofa and mourned the loss of our "girlfriend," as we were fond of calling her. We talked and laughed about things she'd done, habits she'd had, quirks she'd made us used to, great times and loud laughs she'd given us, her antics endearing, her capacity for joy inexhaustible, her passion for life unrelenting.

Lynn reminisced about the early days when Dutchie, as a puppy, resembled a miniature black bear. Back then she was endlessly mischievous. "Remember," Lynn said, "how she bit the heads off my tulips?"

I did.

"Remember," Lynn said, "how she wrecked all the flowers I had started in the planter under my studio window?"

I did.

"Remember," I said, "the day she ran into the back-yard and then into the field and I couldn't catch her and all the neighbors watching from their decks got hysterical?"

Lynn did. We laughed. Even then, at about ten or twelve weeks old, Dutchess was really fast. I had no chance of catching her. Within the year, when she was in Manhattan, I would take her to the dog run beside the Museum of Natural History and she would keep up with the rescued greyhounds as they tore around the perimeter in a racing pack, a canine peloton. Other dog owners would remark to me that she was the fastest Lab they'd ever seen. I knew then nothing about dogs so I couldn't agree or disagree with any authority, even though by that point I was hopelessly in love with her. Actually, I'd been hopelessly in love with her since the first thirty-six hours I spent in her company. I'll tell you all about that in a minute.

First I want to tell you what it's like right now. When Lynn and I finished reminiscing on the sofa tonight, she went up to bed. I usually read or write late into the night. Whenever I did this, Miss Dutchie would always get up from her lair in the kitchen and join me in the living room for a middle-of-the night snack. That is, lately she would do that—for just under the last five years, to be precise, ever since, like a star tailback, she blew out her anterior cruciate ligament, her ACL, and had to have an artificial replacement inserted in her right hind knee. A wizard of a veterinarian named Paul McNamara surgically repaired her knee, but she was never fast again, and she couldn't even climb stairs in comfort. That's how the breakfast nook became her lair; we put twin dog beds in there for her. Before blowing out her ACL she slept in a dog bed beside our bed upstairs. When she was forced after the ACL operation to stay downstairs, neither Lynn nor I ever got used to not hearing her monster sighs in the middle of the night, or her dramatic shifts of position, involving flops and thuds, or her nightmares, in which she would whimper and keen and flail her legs, air-running, escaping her demons.

After Lynn went up to bed I was left downstairs alone. Whenever I went into the kitchen for a decaf refill, I had to remind myself I didn't have to be quiet so as not to wake the Dutchess. Still, as I stood at the counter pouring the coffee, I would glance behind me at her lair. Her black bulk, curled and comfortable, always occupied the corner. Now, momentarily, I was fooled by a dark package of Sure Care underpads sitting where she used to curl up. We needed the underpads after Dutchie's spine gave out and she lost control of all four limbs, her bladder, and her bow-

els. For her last five days of life she was effectively a quad-
riplegic.

The Sure Care underpads sat on the bare quilted foam
rubber of her bed, the cover removed for cleaning. Right
behind the package on the baseboard were the dark stains
deposited there by her bleeding tail. At the end, during
those dreadful last five days she had lost control of everything but her tail. This she could still wag forcefully. With
it for years she used to knock glasses off coffee tables with
ease, so thick and strong was it. For those last five days she
beat her tail so hard against the baseboard that blood and
matted hair congealed on it. Even in the reduced light of
the nighttime kitchen I could see the black bloodstains on
either side of the corner.

Why didn't I clean this up? Why didn't I take people's
advice and throw out everything associated with Dutchie?
Her toys. Her beds. Her bowls. Her leashes. Her water dish.
Her chewed tennis balls. Her car bed. Why didn't I vacuum
up her hair still left in the bathroom in our city apartment?
Why did I stare obsessively at the leg of the sofa in the city
where she used to crouch beside my reading chair? By
rubbing her back against the sofa leg she had worn off part
of the fabric. Whenever I stared at this threadbare spot I
could feel her presence again.

Then again, why did I keep the sympathy card from
the New Baltimore Veterinary Hospital, where she was

euthanized, signed by the veterinarians who always took care of her? And by the veterinarian who euthanized her. Perfunctory though this card was, it was still thoughtful. The vets at New Baltimore, which is in the adjoining town north of Coxsackie, where our upstate house is, had always raved about Dutchie's unbeatably sweet disposition. She always cooperated and never complained.

Why at night in the country did I sometimes go in and look in the little green shopping bag atop the sideboard in the dining room? The little green shopping bag held a cream-colored canister decorated with blue wildflowers. Dutchie's ashes were in the canister. Why couldn't Lynn and I spread these ashes? Why couldn't I, after Dutchie died, instead of having her cremated, bring her body home and bury her in the backyard, as I had always intended to? I couldn't, I just couldn't.

Why was I obsessed with the fate of Barbaro, the Kentucky Derby winner? He was in the University of Pennsylvania's Bolton Center for Large Animals, waiting, I feared, to be euthanized. Crazily I checked the ESPN subscribed news banner for the latest word on him. Religiously I read the news stories on him in *The New York Times* and the *Albany Times-Union*. Fearing he was doomed, I rooted for him maniacally. Just last night on ESPN I learned that Edgar Prado, the great jockey who rode Barbaro to the winner's circle and the garland of roses at Churchill Downs, had gone to visit him that morning, driving six hours round-trip from New York. Prado was currently riding at Belmont. The day after Dutchess was euthanized, Prado had been projected to ride Barbaro to the Triple Crown on June 10, 2006—until Barbaro broke his leg in twenty places running in the Preakness, a fate that would, as I suspected from the beginning, cost him his life eight months later after a gruesome struggle.

I did all of this because I couldn't help myself, I couldn't let go of Miss Dutchie. Of course it was all arguably neurotic. That's the given. Henry James said every book had a given. He high-toned it and used the French word, the *donne*. From this you can tell I was an English major. I'll tell you more about myself, but only incidentally, and only in passing. What I really want to tell you about is Miss Dutchie. Consider this large statement: she taught me more about life than any teacher I ever had. And she never said a word.

If you're the kind of person who takes a dog out behind the barn and puts a slug in the base of its skull when you determine its life is over, and thereby save the dough on any possible vet's bill for euthanization, skip this book. It will only annoy and confuse you. If a dog to you is just another barnyard animal, you won't find anything interesting or extraordinary about Miss Dutchie. But I assure you she was all of that and more.

The day before Dutchess died, a friend in the medical field (for humans) came and looked her over. With the imperious callousness of many people in the medical field, this friend snapped, "Put this animal down."

Next day Miss Dutchie was euthanized. But I never "put her down," a term whose connotations I despise.

In fact this whole book is about raising her up.

CHAPTER TWO

The shortness of her front legs was not the only fault anyone ever found with Dutchess. A psychiatrist friend who lives in our building and owns a rottweiler once remarked to Lynn that Dutchess was "the least aggressive dog I've ever seen." He found her lacking for this. I reveled in it. He also did not see her at the dog run, where she could be patient with suitors until they took too many liberties. I saw her wheel on more than one randy alpha male and back him down. But that was rare and mostly out of character. She was always cheerful, joyous even, and she bounced from one day to the next grinning, playing, strutting, licking and kissing. In New York City she was all *flaneuse,* and made me, for a while, by association, all boulevardier. She lived with us on the Upper West Side and her Broadway strut was magical. She fairly pranced down that wide avenue. Dog lovers would stop her every block. She had an inviting grin about her.

Kids would come straight up to her. I mean really small kids, toddlers who'd just learned to walk, sometimes still doddering a bit. They'd be eye level with her. I would tell her to sit. She would. The kids would pet her face, pat her head, pull her ears, grasp for her swishing tail and yank it if they got hold of it. After asking the parents if it was okay, I would put a dog biscuit in the child's hand and wrap my hand around theirs. Then Dutchie would gently take it, the way Lynn had taught her to, no lunge, no teeth. The kids would squeal with delight and I would assure them they were Dutchess's new best friend. Ever on the con for more food, Dutchess would try for a repeat. Usually she would succeed, especially if there was more than one child present. I wanted each to have the thrill of feeding her.

Of course for Dutchess these walks were exhilarating times. When she was young, robust and mobile, before age enfeebled her, she couldn't wait to get out in the city. An added bonus for her would occur each time Lynn and I could walk her together. Then we three formed a jolly trio. Her energy and excitement infected us as much as it charmed adults and enchanted children. She loved Central Park, but there too, as with overly ardent male suitors in the dog run, her aggressiveness would come out. She loathed squirrels, detested rabbits, and scattered pigeons. The squirrels she treed, the rabbits she holed, and the pigeons she impelled to take wing. Children watching her would squeal with laughter. I knew she would never hurt these animals. Her thing with the birds was the result of hundreds of years of breeding.

The squirrels and rabbits she considered country invaders transplanted to the city. Whenever we drove north from Manhattan up the west side of the Hudson River Valley and arrived late at night at our house in Coxsackie, twenty miles below Albany, the squirrels and rabbits would have invaded our yard. This she considered her domain. As soon as the car stopped I would let her out. For the last three miles she would have been standing in the backseat panting with anticipation anyway. As soon as her feet hit the gravel of the driveway, off she would tear to vanquish all rabbits and squirrels. She would bark beneath the maple tree the squirrels had scrambled up, or she would stalk along the scrub at the edge of the property into which the rabbits had disappeared. Barking was rare for her, and on these occasions I would have to divert her to spare her waking all the neighbors, who, like most country people, retired to bed early.

The way I did this was simple, and proved beyond doubt that I'm simpleminded. I helped her chase the squirrels and rabbits; then, when she started baying and woofing, creating a midnight ruckus, in a loud whisper I'd hiss at her, "She can't catch her uncle." Wheeling, I'd tear off as fast as I could and head for the back of Lynn's studio. Chasing me around the studio was a favorite game we played. As soon as she caught me I'd spin in the opposite direction. In a trice she'd catch me again. Lynn's studio is a converted two-car garage, five hundred square feet, twenty-five feet long by twenty wide. It wouldn't take long for me to be winded. Sometimes I'd still be wearing a suit or a sports coat and slacks from business meetings in the city, and this would inhibit the fun. That's why I tried always to switch into old clothes before we left the city. I would especially try to wear either of two old coats the sleeves of which Dutchess had mangled already, so it wouldn't matter if she mangled them more.

Needing a breather whenever we started this ritual, I'd juke Dutchess till I could round the front of the studio and duck behind the lilac bush and crouch down like a baseball catcher. Immediately she rounded the corner she'd circle the bush and attack, knowing I was there. If I had an old coat on that she'd frayed the sleeve and cuff of already, I would battle her from my catcher's crouch. Lunging, she would clamp on to my cuff or sleeve and pull hard. I would uncoil from my crouch, half stand, and we'd do battle, me in a simian pose like a soccer goalie, arms in a semicircle like giant parentheses, and her ripping into either of my forearms from behind as I constantly pivoted away from her. She would be trying to get a grip and pull or push me over. To thwart her I would pivot, I would twirl. I would egg her on like a chatterbox infielder exhorting his pitcher as Lynn let loose peals of laughter.

This formed our welcome-back-to-the-country ritual. Over the twelve years and two months she lived with us Dutchess and I formed many rituals, all of them fun. Mostly she had to teach them to me, but a few we collaborated on. In the same way we had a separate language, full of loaded phrases that catapulted us into action. "Where's the ball? I can't find the ball" would send her scampering around the house, the apartment, or the yard, depending on wherever I had sounded the alarm. She knew it meant we were going to play. In the city it announced a walk in Central Park. In the dead of winter or in the dead of night in the country it could signal a mad scramble around the dining room table. When that happened sometimes Lynn would join in and we'd try to trap her in pincer movements, but they never worked. She detoured under the dining room table and continued to outflank us with speed. Her broken-field-running ability rivaled an all-American halfback's. Maybe that explained her ruined ACL. She could stop, spin, and shoot off in a new direction in a nanosecond. In the yard this call to fun initiated a throw-and-fetch ritual. I would toss the ball into the back of the yard and she'd retrieve it, often on the first or second bounce— she really was fast.

"Where's that monkey? I can't find the Monkey Man" propelled us into a different game played around the dining room table. Lynn's mother, Frances, who called Dutchess her "granddog," had bought her a stuffed monkey, a chew toy. Dutchess loved it, but as with all her toys, she set out immediately to destroy it. Yet it was fairly indestructible. I would chase her around the dining room table and dive under it and cut her off at the pass and grab one of the monkey's legs. A tug-of-war would result. I would sometimes reel her in and flip her over and she would kick and squirm and twist to escape me, but I would eventually pry the monkey from her. Then I would crawl off with it, back under the table, and she would tear around the table and pin the monkey in my hand as I crawled and then wrench it back from me. I wore out the knees of several pairs of pants this way but Dutchess so loved this game, and so did I, that I didn't care. Also, over the years, the battered monkey had to be sewn up several times by Lynn.

"I'm going to the river. Who wants to go to the river? Where's the ball? I'm leaving, I'm leaving right now" was the supercode. It sent Dutchess into the stratosphere of fun. She was like one of those animals by Chagall floating above the village, swept off the ground, into the air, free for nothing but fun. Our house is a five-minute walk from the Hudson River. We would often take Dutchess down the hill to the riverfront property of our neighbors, the

Warrens. Or, alternatively, depending on whether it was a crowded weekend or an uncrowded weekday, we would treat her to a trip to Riverfront Park in the center of town, on the Coxsackie waterfront. There she loved to run down the boat launch ramp and plunge into the water. When she was young I would throw a tennis ball out forty yards and she would retrieve it numerous times or until, in her excitement, she chomped on it so hard so many times it punctured, took on water, and sank to the bottom. Whenever that happened she'd circle the water where the ball had disappeared for as much as five minutes before I could coax her to shore, such was hundreds of years of breeding frustrated by not retrieving the ball.

If she didn't puncture the ball and lose it, I would hop over the abutment of the boat launch and take off for the open field surrounding the Victorian bandstand in Riverfront Park. She would retrieve the ball, run up the ramp, leap onto the abutment of the launch and sprint after me in fierce pursuit. Then would come the throw-and-fetch game. I would grab the ball from her and hurl it across the field. She would retrieve it endlessly. Sometimes when young children were there, playing or picnicking with their families, they would join in. Dutchess loved to lead them on a merry chase. She reveled in children. No matter what they did to her, from tail pulling to ear yanking, she grinned and gamboled and engaged them in little games that consisted, sometimes, of no more than running in a circle.

I would look up and across the river and see the rolling hills of Columbia County on the other side. In spring they were that magic green that Robert Frost called gold. Darker in summer, they were still beautiful. And then, in fall, would come the riotous, utter magic of golds and reds and russets and yellows. I can remember standing there and watching Dutchess in the foreground and the blue river in the middle ground and the panoply of autumn color in the background and thinking how happy this energetic and life-loving little dog had made me.

Before she showed up I'd had about eight nervous break-downs, major and minor, and a too-close and too-constant acquaintance with clinical depression. I also had a bad case of virulent workaholism and a dose of alcoholism threatening to go rampant.

Miss Dutchie helped arrest, if not cure, almost all of this. But not at first. It took me thirty-six hours to fall in love with her. Then she went to work on me.

CHAPTER THREE

I got Miss Dutchie to get Lynn off my back about my drinking. I paid three hundred dollars for her to a breeder in Athens, New York, the next town south of us in Coxsackie. Nolan Pazin was his name and he was a state trooper, now retired. Nolan had mated Dutchie's mother, a statuesque yellow Lab named Tara, to our neighbor David Gerrain's black Lab named Tar. Tar I knew and loved. He would come visit me in the afternoons after I started treating him to dog biscuits. Tar was something of the canine world's answer to Tom Jones. Gentle, playful, and affectionate, he was, nevertheless, the town stud. His quest for female companionship would send him wandering far and wide. Often I would help his owner, David, retrieve him from the farther environs of the town. We'd ride in a car till we found him.

Other times I'd be somewhere and spot him and coax

him into my Toyota Corolla and drive him home. As Tara was statuesque, Tar was muscular. He looked like a bull-dog in a Lab's body. His affection knew no bounds. When he was scarcely more than a puppy, he would come over and I'd let him in the house and before I knew it he would pin me on the couch and lick my face aerobically. This habit Dutchie inherited from him. And maybe she got the short front legs from him too because her mother was perfect. Tara, though I didn't know it at the time I bought Dutchie, was descended from Governor Averell Harriman's award-winning kennel of Labs. I know this only because Nolan mentioned it to me casually months after I'd bought her.

It all started at a Christmas party at our neighbors the Fenns in 1993. I sidled up to David Gerrain and asked him how my buddy Tar was. David and his wife, Christine, had recently built a new house on the other side of town, so Tar wasn't around as frequently as he used to be. Still, David's parents, Frank and Janet, lived right across the road from us and I'd discover Tar in the backyard or on our deck from time to time. His romantic rambles would bring him back to the old neighborhood, called the Hill, and he would drop in on me as well as spend time with his grand-parents, so to speak. I missed him. Lynn and I also missed Suzie, a female black Lab who had belonged to our next-door neighbors Pete and Lois Cameron.

Suzie had contracted severe diabetes and had to be euthanized, of all times, during Christmas week of 1992. For the first five years that we owned our house Suzie had been our weekend dog. Pete and Lois used to joke that she was more our dog than theirs during the weekends. Lynn had practically adopted Suzie. A farm girl, Lynn loved animals. While growing up in Middleburg, Pennsylvania, she had had dogs for pets and she used to be especially thrilled to go to the livestock sales at the Auction Barn on the edge of town with her dad and her granddad. She has an eye for animals and loves them. She's made us money at the track watching the horses in the paddock before a race and then having me place a last-minute bet on her choice. Anyway, when she co-opted Suzie, Pete and Lois were so gracious they joked about it. On weekends Suzie fell into the habit of camping outside Lynn's studio all day, thirty feet behind our house, where Lynn drew and painted.

I feared dogs and disliked animals. Unlike Lynn, I had grown up in the inner city, in North Philadelphia. Dogs there were often threatening. There was the police K-9 Unit, of course, but there were also guard dogs at places like the coal yard and Joe the Junkie's. Joe had nothing to do with drugs. He bought old newspapers and scrap iron and other salvageable material before anyone ever heard the term *recycle*. These guard dogs tended to be German shepherds and Dobermans and they weren't warm and cuddly. Also, in North Philly people's pet dogs often doubled as additions to their arsenals, combat ready. Kids liked to hiss, "Sic him, boy, sic him," when disputes got heated, and a dog attacking somebody was far from unheard of. For this purpose the black kids favored Chow dogs, the white kids German shepherds, and when the odd small-scale race riot threatened to erupt over dibs on the use of the ball field or the basketball court, a Chow or a German shepherd would often cast the deciding vote.

This fear of dogs was so ingrained in me I remember one night in the late eighties walking up West End Avenue with Lynn and our friends Bill Shinker and Susan Moldow. Susan spotted a guy coming toward us with a pit bull on a leash and stopped when he reached us and asked if she could pet his dog. As she did, I stood rooted, braced, all but digging my heels in but for our being on a concrete sidewalk. I was certain Susan was about to lose a hand, especially from all I'd heard about pit bulls, but of course she didn't.

Still, I didn't favor dogs and didn't fancy owning one. I didn't even relate to Lassie or to Rin Tin Tin on TV in my boyhood or, reading in grade-school anthologies, to "A Boy and His Dog" stories, or to Shaggy Dog stories of any kind. I didn't read children's classics featuring animals because there was no children's literature in my house. In high school *The Red Pony* left me cold. This is a serious deficiency on my part, granted, but it took the arrival of Miss Dutchie and half a century for me to find it out.

Darling Suzie Cameron initiated the process. She loved being around Lynn on weekends and, before long, she started coming over to me when I came outside to see Lynn or to jog. Lynn had laid in a supply of dog biscuits for Suzie and in short time I was feeding them to her as well. In the early days of owning the house Lynn and I used it only on weekends because we had to work in the city during the week, me in book publishing, her teaching art and design in college. I loved to jog and suddenly one day when I came out to jog in the country Suzie jumped up from her station beside the door to Lynn's studio and came with me.

This amused me. In those days I trained even on the country hills at eight-minute miles, but this speed didn't faze Suzie. In fact the opposite was true. She could have left me standing at any time. Instead she geared down and stayed right with me except for the occasional dash into the fields to smell another animal's scent. Our house is on a tertiary road that dead-ends about a mile and a half away at Swezey's farm.

Right before you reach the farm you can jog down an incline and reach a strip of sand when the Hudson's tide is out. On our first jog together Suzie shot ahead and down this incline. I followed her through the underbrush out onto the strip of sand and watched as she dashed into the river. She swam out and then came back and jumped up at me. She grabbed a stick and taunted me with it. I knew enough to pull it from her and wing it as far into the river as I could. She tore off and swam after it. This routine repeated itself. I struggled with her mightily when she brought back the stick after a frantic swim. She adored a tug-of-war. Sand would fly. She would take flying leaps at me, ears pinned back, eyes flashing. Often I would fall backward, still clutching the stick and tussling with her for it as I fought to regain my footing. She loved it. I loved it.

Next thing I knew I was talking to her. I was talking to a dog. This practice I had always looked askance at. It stuck me as decadent, a rich people's indulgence. The neighborhood I grew up in in North Philly, Fairmount, abuts Fairmount Park where it edges up against the art museum. Directly across from the entrance to the park sits the 2601 Parkway apartment building, quite upscale. As kids we passed on its wide sidewalks on our way to and from St. Francis Xavier grammar school and to and from Roman Catholic High School. The residents of the "Oh-One," as it was called, would walk their poodles and spaniels, their Pekingese and their dachshunds, their Chihuahuas and terriers on these broad sidewalks.

The owners would be dripping jewels or wrapped in furs, and the dogs themselves would have little winter outfits and tiny blankets, or, in summer, bows and little bonnets complementing rhinestone collars and leashes and assorted nonsense like that. It wasn't rare for a lapdog to be carried outside on an embroidered pillow by a uniformed maid or one of the doormen in quasi-military drag. Often the owners would be chattering away to their charges. They would even nuzzle them and kiss them right on the muzzle. This we mocked. The retort, from the "rich people," as we called them, was to berate us as "JDs," which was short for *juvenile delinquents*. Very fifties, that. Remember: This was the era of *The Blackboard Jungle* and *West Side Story* and, on television, great actors like George C. Scott in *Naked City* corralling incorrigibles on brownstone stoops in Hell's Kitchen or East Harlem.

When Suzie contracted diabetes and had to be euthanized at only seven and a half years old, it left a big hole in Lynn's heart. She cried profusely when Pete Cameron invited us to his house next door to say goodbye to her. I stood there stunned. Emotionally frozen, as usual. But I had awful feelings coursing through me, powerful feelings. Yet I was able to deny and contain them. I maintained my composure and we left. This was in the late afternoon of a dreary December day and dusk fell soon afterward. I found myself staring through the big bay window in our living room when full darkness arrived. Pete and Lois's house is visible from our living room across a wide expanse of their lawn.

Pete had said he would take Suzie to the vet's at five thirty. Pete's garage is visible from our living room and has a sensor light above it. I saw him come out with Suzie and leave, and then I watched until he returned about half an hour later. He took from the bed of his pickup a bundle wrapped in a blanket and went around to the back of his house. Pete himself died three years later of cancer. He was a fantastic man, and I was honored to speak at his memorial service. At the service his incredibly beautiful widow, Lois, explained that Pete had always said his religion was nature and his cathedral the great outdoors. I liked that.

Pete grew up on a farm in Coxsackie during the Great Depression. He loved to garden and kept a big truck garden behind his house each summer. From it he kept us supplied with tomatoes, squash, broccoli, beans, mush melons, cantaloupes, and watermelons. "Generous" doesn't begin to describe Pete. At his memorial service, Lois said Pete wanted his ashes scattered over the back of his property, where he kept his garden. It looks out on the Catskills in the distance. He had told me earlier that leaden and dreary December afternoon that he would bury Suzie there when he brought her home that evening from the New Baltimore Animal Hospital.

He did. I told myself that's that. But it wasn't.

CHAPTER FOUR

I miss a lot. I've always had an intense interior life and sometimes I muse and that's how I miss a lot. I fatally don't care about too much stuff: cars, clothes, houses, jewelry, chic restaurants, power and prestige, titles and positions, money and net worth. For a while in my publishing career I vaguely cared about such things but not enough. I realize I'm indifferent to mundane possessions and earthly success. Since grade school I wanted to write, in high school it took hold of me, and in college, and ever since, it has obsessed me. I've also never been hip and couldn't care less. Being a square is okay with me. In the sixties there was an iconic, for me, Charlie Brown cartoon. In it Charlie lamented that every time he found out "where it was at," they "moved it." I was like that but I didn't care. I had too much going on in my own head to overvalue exterior reality or what went on in it.

A lot of writers and artists are like this. So too are a lot of alcoholics. There is also a lot of overlap between the two sets. In both cases their interior monologue is loud and intense. When you throw in a smidgen of schizophrenia, as happened to me in my late twenties and early thirties, and the monologue goes duologue or multilogue, you got problems, especially if you vocalize the voices and start a question-and-answer volley. Often this marks what the shrinks call a "separation from reality." Talk then about missing a lot and you're into serious understatement.

So when Suzie died I missed it that I'd lost my first dog. Lynn didn't miss it and that formed the genesis of Dutchess.

I was tickled back then whenever my buddy Tar showed up for dog bones and a rubdown. He would lick my face as I sat with him on the deck or crouched down to pet him in the kitchen. In winter I gave him the run of the house, so he could warm up between his peregrinations looking for female companionship. By this time, early 1993, I had left my job as publisher in New York and retreated to the country to write a novel. I worked in my upstairs study and whenever Tar came over it was a bonus break, a fun-filled interlude. His presence would remind me how much I missed Suzie, but I'd shrug it off and go back to work.

Lynn didn't shrug it off. She started to talk about how much she missed Suzie. Counting college, she had lived dogless in cities—first in Philadelphia and then in Manhattan—for twenty-six years at that point, ever since she'd left home in central Pennsylvania. She started to lobby me for a dog and to dog me about my drinking. By then she had hounded me enough that I'd joined AA but I didn't take it seriously at first. It would take seven more years before that happened, from 1991 to 1998. Initially I thought AA was a cliché-ridden cult for kooks, wimps, and losers. Lynn was raised Protestant and I thought she was having a Carry Nation Anti-Saloon League seizure. AA I also considered a Protestant-driven puritanical campaign to short-circuit my God-given right as a high-spirited, high-energy Irishman to roister the night away and to bay at the moon if the mood struck me.

On all counts I was wrong. With hangovers I felt guilty. Whether the result of Catholicism or not, the most overdeveloped organ in my body is my conscience. My psychiatrist marvels at how easy it is to make me feel guilty. Once I cracked him up by retorting that maybe I was the opposite of a sociopath, a kind of consciopath. Instead of being unable to recognize right from wrong maybe it was the only thing I could discern.

The upshot was this: A year after Suzie died I bought Dutchess sight unseen at that 1993 Christmas party at our neighbors' Danny and Lianne Fenn. Danny and Lianne are Pete and Lois's son-in-law and daughter. I casually asked fellow guest David Gerrain how my good buddy Tar was and whether David had any plans to breed him. As a matter of fact he just had. He told me about Nolan Pazin and his beautiful yellow female Lab named Tara. I asked how much the puppies cost. For three hundred dollars on impulse I bought Dutchie on the spot. All I specified, mindful of Suzie, was that I wanted a black female. Suzie had been no wanderer like Tar and I didn't fancy chasing all over the neighborhood reining in a randy male.

I said not a word about this to Lynn. David told me the litter was due in late February. The ideal time to take ownership of a puppy, he said, was at about seven weeks. That meant Dutchess would be ready to come live with us in mid-April. Since Lynn's birthday is March 19, I figured I'd tell her that her gift was out of stock but would be in in a few weeks.

That's what I did, but a wave of doubt hit me. How would we cope with a dog with our crowded schedules? How would we transport the dog back and forth between the country and the city? Did some dogs hate riding in cars? I didn't know even this basic thing about dogs. I knew some dogs tore up furniture and wrecked houses. Would we get that kind of dog? Would the dog like the city? I'd never had Tar or Suzie in the city with me. A lot of questions crowded in on me and doubts assailed me but I was decisive to a fault and I wanted more than anything to make Lynn happy. Her happiness is supremely important to me and has been for four decades.

I also wanted to make up to her for my awful propensity to dipsomania, especially of late when my writing was frustrating me on a weekly basis, prompting my thirst to intensify. And, as I mentioned, I wanted to get Lynn off my back about this increased tippling, as I still blithely but foolishly thought of it.

So here came Dutchess.

CHAPTER FIVE

Dutchess was born on February 24, 1994, one of two black females in a litter of eight. I have a mind like a berserk chronometer and I later worked back to what I was doing that day, with the help of journal notes. I got a haircut at the Hudson Plaza across the river in Hudson and bought a cheap red shirt I liked at Ames, of all places. I think that night I called my great boyhood buddy Joey Mastrangelo and wished him a happy birthday, but I was unaware Tara had dropped her litter so I didn't tease him that he shared a birthday with my dog, something I would do in later years that made us both laugh. Otherwise that day I didn't know what I was up to other than working away on my novel and hitting, reluctantly, grudgingly, the odd AA meeting.

But I had started to ask questions of friends about what actually owning a dog entailed. That's how I learned what to do on the day I was to pick Dutchess up. Bring a box, they said, with an old towel in it and an old shoe for the puppy to chew. Then one dark cold night in late March David Gerrain called to ask if I wanted to go see the litter. I did. We went down to Nolan Pazin's house in Athens and there in the basement was the whole litter jockeying for position on Tara's swollen teats in a big box filled with shredded newspaper.

The puppies were tiny, about four weeks old. David asked permission of Nolan and picked one of the two black females up. She fitted easily in his open hand. With my index finger I stroked her. There's a fifty percent chance she was Dutchess. Truth to tell I was a little put off and stunned by what I'd done in buying a dog and the whole excursion made me a little nervy. The puppies were so needy and so eager to crawl over and around one another and suckle their mother's teats that the scene was a bit too barnyard for me. The panicky thought that I'd made an impulsive mistake shot through me. But Lynn would love a puppy, I told myself, so shut up.

When Nolan asked me which female I wanted, I told him, "Just give me the one you don't want." Why be picky when I didn't have a clue what I was doing anyway? I thanked Nolan and his wife, Connie, for showing me the puppies, and David and I left. Nolan had said he'd call David when the puppies were weaned, in a few weeks, and I could come back and pick ours up. So the whole thing was really going to happen. I drove home with David and thought no more about it till he called on April 12 and told me Nolan said to pick up my puppy the next evening, after work. The whole next day I was excited and I welcomed the chance to have lunch with my friend John Lees, a painter who lives a few towns away in Leeds with his painter wife, Ruth Leonard, the most passionate dog lover I've ever met. John and I talked and laughed the afternoon away and I left his house in the early evening and drove to Nolan's house in Athens.

Before I knew it I had paid the three hundred dollars and Nolan had pressed Dutchess into my arms. She squirmed and squealed and didn't like it. She nipped at my hands. I took her out to our car, a silver Toyota Corolla hatchback, put her in the box I'd brought with the old towel and shoe in it, thanked Nolan and Connie, and drove out of their driveway. No sooner did I start down the road than Dutchess let loose. She squealed and screamed and climbed out of the box, which I had placed on the passenger seat.

Driving with one hand, I tried to calm her and keep her in the box. Her response was to climb my forearm, yapping and nipping, and panicking left, right, and center. I am not a typically helpless male. As the second oldest of twelve children, I had eight younger sisters and two younger brothers. I am over sixteen years older than my baby sister Sally. I had minded children, babysat them, and diapered and powdered infants. I knew how to watch infants so they didn't roll off the table when you diapered them, I had accidentally stuck myself many times with pins so I wouldn't stick the babies while diapering the old-fashioned, pre-Velcro way, and I had burped more infants than many maternity ward nurses.

Still, driving on a secondary rural road, Route 385, which connects Coxsackie and Athens, while trying to calm a cosmologically panicked Labrador retriever puppy seven weeks old taxed me hard. I drove slowly. I tried baby talk, I tried lullabies, I swerved over the line, I swerved back, I slowed down way below the limit of fifty-five miles an hour. Nothing worked: I failed to calm her. With every rotation of the wheels taking her away from Tara and her siblings Dutchess seemed to panic more. Sweat popped out on my forehead. My mouth went dry. I pushed her back into the box and tried to pet her to calm her, like a nurse stroking a patient's cheek, but before I could do this she would be halfway up my forearm, scraping her little nails on me and nipping at me with needlelike teeth. The ride was only seven miles but they were the longest and hardest seven miles I've ever driven, and it took us more than twice as long as normal to reach home. When we got into our driveway I thought I'd made it. The worst had to be over, I figured.

I was mistaken. It was about six o'clock on a Tuesday evening. Lynn wasn't due back from the city until the late train on Thursday night. I had bought dog food and dog treats and a big, comfortable crate and had set it up in the kitchen, near the breakfast nook. It was this breakfast nook that would become, years later, Dutchie's lair. I took Dutchie out of the box in the car and brought her into the kitchen and placed her in the crate. I closed it and felt like I'd managed the really hard part. I would work on my novel upstairs and this cute little ball of fur of a black Labrador puppy would snooze away downstairs in her big, roomy, comfortable, and expensive crate.

I was on the ball. I put a little dish of water in the crate and the old shoe for her to chew. She was watching me intently. I gave her a little puppy biscuit. I touched her through the wire mesh of the crate. I would check on her every now and again, I figured, whenever I came downstairs for a decaf refill, which is what I drank all day periodically after a little caffeinated coffee in the morning. Otherwise the caffeine made me too jumpy. I wondered if there was anything else I should do for the puppy. I didn't want to be accused by Lynn or anyone else of dereliction of duty. Some people had told me to put a ticking clock in the crate but that seemed ridiculous and I didn't.

I started out of the kitchen and she let out an ungodly squeal.

My mother, who knew a lot about babies, used to say that crying was an infant's only form of exercise. Kicking the air and flailing with the arms, fists clenched, did them good. It tired them, they fell asleep. I thought this same approach likely applied to puppies as well. Dutchess would howl a bit like an infant, then drop off into a deep and peaceful sleep.

I started up the stairs to my study to write. With each step I took, Dutchess seemed to scream and thrash, cry and squeal, howl and yap louder and louder. "Sometimes," I could hear my mother's voice say, "you have to ignore a baby for its own good. Let them have a good cry. They'll fall asleep exhausted and sleep well."

I went in my study and sat at my computer. I listened to Dutchie carrying on downstairs. My concern grew. Despite this I booted up my computer. I had done my Harold Lloyd imitation driving her home on Route 385. She was in the house, she was safe. I could safely pursue the dream I'd left book publishing to realize and write my novel. I loved to write to the sounds of soft jazz or classical playing on the stereo. I debated putting a CD on but decided Coltrane or Ellington or Beethoven would be irresponsible right now. I knew from tons of experience you had to listen for babies, to ensure their welfare. That too must hold true, I speculated, for puppies. Besides, Dutchess downstairs was setting up a crescendo of escalating pain so loud it would ruin the music even if I put it on.

I tried to write and lasted less than five minutes. Dutchess was in ontological pain. She panicked, I panicked. I had to comfort her. I couldn't stand it. I didn't know it but, this side of a full psychotic break, I was about to live through the most stressful fifty hours of my life. Chauffeur by Harold Lloyd was about to give way to wet nurse by Martin Short.

CHAPTER SIX

Nothing I did calmed her. She was a bundle of black fur, anger, and neediness. The only thing I could think of was that my little brothers and sisters used to stop squealing when you picked them up and strolled around the room, patting them on the back and cooing. When kneeling down and talking softly through the wire mesh of the crate didn't work, I called Ruth Leonard and explained that the puppy was completely panicked and out of control. She suggested I try something. I got an empty can and filled it with pennies. This I rattled as loud as I could while kneeling beside the crate. The louder the can rattled the louder Dutchess screamed. After about fifteen minutes I called Ruth back and told her it wasn't working. She said it would work eventually, just keep it up. I did. Half an hour later nothing had changed except my wrist was sore.

So I opened the crate, pulled Dutchess out, and started

to stroll around the first floor, looping from the kitchen to the living room and then into the dining room. There I would circle the dining room table several times, cradling her, cooing to her, stroking her chin or patting her back, depending upon which configuration she had wiggled and contorted herself into against my chest or shoulders. She never held one position for more than a minute. Finally, after an eternity of wailing and screeching, she subsided. The racket briefly ceased. Tired and relieved, I noticed that her eyes were closed. This touched me. She was angelic. She nestled in my arms, her face against my chest, mouth drooling. I went into the living room and sat in my favorite club chair next to the fireplace, leaned my head back and closed my eyes. This stillness sparked a new explosion. Dutchie went off again, squealing and squirming and climbing up my chest and arms. Then she pissed all over me.

A pattern was set. For the next thirty-six hours she would keep me on my toes. All my negotiations with her were to no avail. To quiet her I popped up and paced the first floor again, resuming my loops of the dining room table. Briefly she quieted, then she would nod off. I would tiptoe into the living room, humming softly, usually lullabies I had conjured from memory, stored three decades but now useful again. I could hear my mother singing them to me and to my brothers and sisters. I was humming "The Muffin Man" and singing the "Patty Cake Baker's Man" song. I changed the "B" for "Baby" to a "D" for "Dutchie" in the final line, so the song went: "Bakerman, Bakerman, bake me a cake as fast as you can/ Roll it and pat it and mark it with a D/ and put it in the oven for Dutchie and me."

She didn't care for it, Dutchie didn't. My singing is generally unpopular. My voice is pitched something like Howdy Doody with laryngitis. So every time I tiptoed in and settled in the club chair next to the fireplace, put my head back and closed my eyes, she would come to, startled, and let out a blast. Her anger grew, my irritation increased. Finally I decided to hell with this and I put her in the crate and went upstairs to write. I had abandoned my career in Manhattan as an editor and publisher to write a novel and that is what I would do.

I went into my study, put some jazz on the CD player, and settled down to write. Over the soothing jazz I could hear her screaming downstairs. All my life I had read such palaver as the assertion that real writers let nothing interfere with their writing. Their destiny as scribes is all that matters. I told myself that is how I had to be now. I booted up the computer and started to review the pages I had written at my last session. I tried to ignore Dutchie and her fear. I failed and rationalized that if I brought her upstairs into my study she would calm down. I went down and got her and carried her up to my study. I put her down on the rug and resumed staring at my computer screen, pondering what immortal prose to commit to the key-board.

She screeched away. Although my study has three nice windows I had placed my computer against a blank wall in a Bartleby-like homage to my own seriousness. Behind me on the floor in front of the built-in bookshelves that lined one wall sat the partial typescript of my novel. I stared, Dutchie squealed. I recalled yet again my mother saying crying was good for babies. It was exercise and all that. I ignored Dutchie. She came to the base of my office chair and wailed up at me. I ignored her. I looked at my computer screen and knew my nerves were shot, to bor-row a favorite expression of my mother's, now quaint and Victorian, like many of her vivid Irish locutions, most of them also now passing out of the language. Just as I had always done with my younger siblings when I caved in to their pain and picked them up, I turned in the chair, re-solved to pick up Dutchie and comfort her.

Immediately I spotted several wet spots on the rug and, worse, looking up, I spied Dutchie crouched on the partial typescript of my novel. Before my mouth fell open all the way she took a dump on the pile of typescript. I made a resigned kind of *uuuhhh* sound as she squirted a stream of urine on the script for good measure before stepping off it, keening for all she was worth. That was it for me. To hell with owning a dog. To hell with surprising Lynn with this darling little living creature for a birthday present. I was bound and determined to write my novel and I was damned if I was going to let a dog short-circuit my long-delayed dream. I closed the door to my study on Dutchie and tromped downstairs and called the breeder, the wonderful state trooper who'd sold her to me, Nolan Pazin.

When he answered I told him he could have the puppy back and he could keep the three hundred bucks I'd paid for her. I told him she was having a sustained nervous breakdown away from her mother and her littermates and it was the cruelest thing I'd ever witnessed. I didn't tell him that I now understood in horrifying new ways the agony of family breakups as routine as those from divorce and as catastrophic as those from forced emigration or from wartime displacement. I did say that Dutchie needed to be restored to the big box in his basement and given away to some deserving youngster at the proper time for her to endure this savage separation from her mother and her siblings. That time was clearly not now. The deserving youngster, unlike me, would probably even know how to calm and console a puppy.

He laughed. He told me all puppies went through this process. In a few days, he assured me with a chuckle, that little puppy would adore me. "I said to my wife, 'Connie, that man will be the best owner any of them in this litter gets,'" he stated, very matter-of-fact, deadpan. When I met him I had liked him immediately. He had that steadiness you get in some military officers and police officers that is very reassuring to others in emergencies, that unflappable quality they often have that I so admire. That was only one reason I had so liked working with my military guys and gals as an editor and publisher. They were usually steady and not so touchy and temperamental as a lot of writers tend to be. I said to Nolan, "She's also a biter. She's nipped me several times. My fingers have bled." I would bet my eyeteeth that at this statement he wanted to roar with laughter, but he was too kind to do it. He didn't even chuckle.

I am as citified as a manhole cover or a cockroach, and country people have been very tolerant of me on this score all the time I've lived in Coxsackie. Writing this fact down here I feel compelled to add that my wife is country people too, and she's certainly been tolerant of me and my citified ways and my ignorance of country life and country realities. One day this monstrous turtle was crossing Riverside Avenue where we live and I stopped the car in awe to watch its progress. It was the size of a car tire laid on its side. It moved slowly. I watched and wondered if I should get out and pick it up and put it at the side of the road so no reckless driver ran over it. But I sat there watching, fascinated, instead. It was the kind of turtle they say is a remnant of a dinosaur. It was a terrapin, I think, like the mascot of the

University of Maryland, and it was headed toward the river, about two hundred yards away. When I got home and told Lynn I almost got out and picked it up, she gasped. "Never do that," she shrieked, "it'll snap the tops of your fingers off. It'll crush 'em." This sent a chill through me. How was I going to type a classic novel with the tips of my fingers gone?

But, right then that first night with Dutchie, what was enraging me was how I was going to be a writer with this feral puppy disrupting my sacrosanct writing time. I couldn't go into all these particulars on the phone with Nolan Pazin. Even I knew I sounded ridiculous. He wasn't a chatterbox, Mr. Pazin, as I called him, but he started to tell me that this phase would pass quickly. It was only "panic until she gets used to you. Wait till she gets accustomed to you and she'll be fine," he added. He reviewed with me a few things he'd told me earlier that evening when I picked Dutchie up. I was to make sure I kept taking her out in the yard to relieve herself so she'd get the idea not to go indoors. I almost snapped back at him that I already had a rug full of piss rings and a typescript used as a latrine but I had been going to AA meetings and the great thing I was learning, with monumental reluctance, was "restraint of tongue and pen."

Besides, he couldn't have been nicer on the phone. I hung up convinced he hadn't sold me a bill of goods. I mean, for God's sake, he could have taken the puppy back, pocketed my three hundred smackers, resold her, and doubled his profits. Instead he consoled me and told me this was just a bad patch and it would pass quickly. I had thanked him, put the phone down, and sat in my fireside chair smoking a cigarette. Since I'd picked Dutchie up earlier that evening I'd had no chance to have a puff. There'd been no peace. What's more, I didn't yet know that in the future whenever I did light up Dutchie was going to scream worse from the cigarette smoke as though it were pepper spray I was exhaling. Now I had to figure out how to get the urine stains out of the rug. I didn't yet know about Carbona and Renew and the other pet stain removers, but oh, was I going to learn about them.

Sitting in the living room I dragged on my cigarette like Jimmy Cagney having his last smoke before entering the gas chamber, but with no Pat O'Brien to clasp me on the shoulder and whisper, "Be brave, my son, it will all be over soon and you'll be with God in heaven." The whole time I smoked I listened to Dutchie raising hell upstairs in my study.

I was split right down the middle. As someone trying to get permanently off booze I had lost my favorite recreational tranquilizer. So I had to sit there and cold turkey deal with rage at myself for getting this puppy in the first place and possibly wrecking my chance to finally write a serious novel. In early sobriety, rage can be a huge issue. Lynn had been making unpleasant noises about anger management courses. I hated her New Age awareness of such stuff. In fact right then I blamed this AA boondoggle on her too. I had an impulse to drive into town and buy two six-packs of Coors Light and a pint of Johnnie Walker Black Label and let this screaming pooch wear herself out. But the other side of me, the side that was one of twelve children, none of whom got enough attention or affection growing up, since that was impossible given our numbers; plus the side of me that had suffered debilitating bouts of clinical depression and what are commonly called nervous breakdowns; augmented, finally, by the side of me that wanted to be comforted and calmed—all of these sides of me took hold.

I crushed the cigarette butt out in the big glass ashtray on the washstand next to my chair. Here in this chair was where I read myself tired in the lonely nights smoking away with the fireplace crackling. This chair was, according to my wife, "my nest." Had I now ruined this bucolic idyll, writing a novel by day, reading by the fire at night, taking it easy, being what I asininely thought of as literary?

I mounted the stairs to my study determined not, like my parents, to show that puppy who was boss, but to show that puppy who could be grown-up and loving, who could be affectionate and comforting and who could vanquish her existential panic.

I also had to get the dog turds off my typescript and out of my study.

How could I know then that Dutchie was simply preparing me for the critical reception my novel would meet with over the years as I endured thirtysomething turndowns from editors and publishers?

Old Dutchie was into literary foreshadowing big time.

She knew worlds more about life, too, and over the next twelve years and two months she was going to teach it all to me.

But right then I was just annoyed, angry, and weirdly determined to subdue her by placating her, by reassuring her, by loving her, to show her who really understood the need for love and the basics of psychology: animal, plant, or human.

CHAPTER SEVEN

Grief is ubiquitous, loss is awful. Two nights ago on the Trailways bus roaring up the New York Thruway from Manhattan to Kingston, I woke in time to look up and spot the Medina rest stop on the opposite side of the road. At the north end of the parking lot I saw the tractor-trailers pulled up into the area reserved for them. Right in front of it is a little triangle of grass where motorists allow their dogs to roam and relieve themselves. I used to stand there sucking on a cigarette while Dutchie did her business, sometimes in gruesomely cold weather, often beside twelve-foot-high piles of dirty snow and ice deposited there by the front-loaders that cleared the parking lot. The spot was magical for Dutchie. She would smell, smell, smell. It was almost as good in that respect as New York City itself. All the other dogs would have left their calling cards and Dutchie felt compelled to get a whiff of every single one. But she would always come promptly on my second definitive call because I'd learned early on to lure her with dog biscuits from what she considered Scent Heaven.

She would jump into the backseat of the car and I would put a biscuit between my front teeth and turn to her. She would lean forward and snare it, surgically, without touching my lips. I would protest that she'd stolen my biscuit and her tail would whip around frantically, beating a rhythm off the backseat cushions like Gene Krupa on a roll. Then I'd repeat the process and she'd snatch the biscuit cleanly again and mock my faux indignation with a celebratory tail tattoo off those same battered cushions.

What I'm trying to say is that when you lose a pet everything reminds you of that loss, or so it seems. When the bus got to Kingston that night Dutchie was no longer there pulling against the leash as Lynn held her back at the steps leading off the bus. And then there were all the little reminders: you no longer had heaps of empty dog food cans to take to the recycling station with the trash on Saturdays; you no longer checked to make sure her collar was on before heading for the city; you no longer had to vacuum every other day so you weren't overrun with dog hair; you no longer had to bathe her, brush her hair, make sure she took her heartworm pill—it was endless, this daily assault of reminders that she was no longer there and that her absence was killing you.

But that first night she came to live with us I would have given her away for a plugged nickel. When I got back upstairs to my study she was in full meltdown. She was rambling around the room and taking sporadic leaks as she squatted and squirted every few steps. She kept coming to my legs and trying to climb them. I sat down in my club chair in the study next to my freestanding bookshelf and tried to have a little think. One of my chief flaws, and I have plenty of them, is impatience.

Yet it was clear to me from what Nolan Pazin had counseled that I should forget writing on this night and concentrate on caring for this puppy. It would be the only way to calm her down. Impulsively and stupidly, in an act of total avoidance, I fired up another cigarette. She climbed my shins as I sat and smoked. She seemed further enraged by the foul smoke and I thought again what a pig's habit smoking cigarettes is. But I continued to smoke mine to the tune of two to two and a half packs a day. Defiance and addiction are twin columns in my pantheon of shortcomings. When I finished this latest smoke I crushed out the butt and stared down at her where she squealed.

Then I picked her up and cuddled her against my chest and she calmed herself briefly, though she did not stop squirming on my chest and digging those tiny nails on her paws into the fabric of my shirt, slicing tiny little tears into it. I patted her on my shoulder as I might have burped a baby and soon I felt a warm dollop of urine spread against my shirt in front of my left nipple. I thought I should call Lynn in the city and ask her advice. By now it was eight o'clock and I realized she'd soon be home from teaching her courses at the School of Visual Arts. But if I did that I would ruin her birthday surprise. As I mentioned, I had told Lynn I had ordered her gift but it was out of stock.

I decided I would get a sponge from under the kitchen sink downstairs and a little Woolite rug cleaner and see what I could do about cleaning up. I wondered how many pages of my typescript her poop and pee had penetrated and how many I'd have to print out fresh. I stared at my typescript as Dutchie had newly decorated it and, though a professed atheist at times, I silently prayed that I had not made a catastrophic blunder in bringing this little animal home to live with us. When I put her down to go get the sponge and the Woolite she went ballistic and made sure I had even more to clean up.

As you can see by now, perspective is not my long suit either.

I went downstairs and got the sponge and the rug cleaner. When I got back to my study and set to work cleaning up, Dutchie made a royal nuisance of herself. Whether I was on my knees or on all fours, she attacked me as I attacked the stains, climbing my forearms, scratching and screeching, running underfoot whenever I attempted to change positions and sanitize a new stain. She tumbled under me and generally exasperated me. But I did finish the stains I could see. The room had a slight odor of urine, but it was overpowered by the stench of her feces. So I got paper towels and cleaned that mess up. Then I looked mournfully at my desecrated typescript and cursed Dutchie mildly under my breath. The soothing jazz on the CD player had long since expired. I clicked it off, took a few last swipes at the room, cracked the window slightly to disperse the odors, and picked the obstreperous Dutchie up, tucked her bucking and squirming in the crook of my arm and toted her downstairs like a dogcatcher about to condemn her to the pound.

In my other hand I had the Woolite and the sponge and the befouled paper towels and their contents, Dutchie's droppings. I had swiped at the soggy top pages of my type-script but I decided that was the least of my worries for the moment. My moods were swinging wider and faster than Poe's pendulum. One minute I was enraged at this ball of fur scratching and biting my forearm, the next I was vow-ing tenderness toward her sufficient to satiate even the most lovelorn heart. And through it all I was feeling like a trapped submariner on the ocean floor with the supply of oxygen running out, my overactive imagination fueling the fantasy that the oxygen running out for me was the rapidly dissipating chance that I would be able to write my long anticipated novel, straight and serious, unlike the genre men's adventure novels I'd written under a pseud- onym years earlier. I had so hoped those novels would sell well enough to grant me the time and money to retreat to a simple cabin on, say, Prince Edward Island and there create, from chilly April to nippy October, a little gem of a serious novel I'd be forever proud of that, by dint of ge- nius, would win me the Nobel Prize for Literature. Such was my wayward thinking fueled by outlandish fantasy.

I had always laughed at what I pretentiously called the bourgeoisie whenever I was in my Jimmy Porter moods, looking back, and forward, and sideways, in anger. I could see the silly bejeweled and befurred old ladies with blue hair back in Fairmount delicately picking up after their lapdogs in front of the 2601 apartment building opposite the art museum. In my mind's eye I saw them dab oh so demurely at their rugrat's tuchus, and smirked with con- tempt at myself now for picking up after a dog, a frenzied puppy the same size as their obnoxious pooches. I was not reassured about myself to realize that, like an eccentric vicar in an English mystery on A&E, I had been talking, even baby-talking, to this diminutive creature under my arm who was disrupting my house, blighting my writing career, and demolishing what little mental equilibrium I had left, which was precious little after two decades in the book publishing business.

In the kitchen I put Dutchess down on the floor as I stood at the sink cleaning up. She attempted to scale my calves. I turned and snatched her up and then deposited her back in her wire mesh crate. I thought, as I closed the crate door on her, *If I get rid of her, I lose the eighty bucks on the crate, too. What was I thinking when I came up with this grand scheme to make Lynn deliriously happy?* I bound all the stinky stuff up in plastic bags, sealed them, and took them down to the big trash cans in the cellar. Standing in the coolness of the damp cellar, staring at the stone foundation, more than a century and a half old, I thought these walls and stones and boards of this late Federalist house had withstood a lot more over that span of time than Dutchess's rage.

Upstairs I could hear her thrashing against the wire mesh, raising a helluva racket, squealing and screaming and baying and mewling and tempting me with the thought of stalking upstairs and wringing her neck like a spring chicken. No sooner did I think this than I excoriated myself for thinking it. Instead the urge to tenderness overwhelmed me again. I climbed the stairs quickly, took her out of the crate, and started to stroll around the first floor caressing her while cooing to her.

When I had called Nolan Pazin earlier and offered to return her without getting my money back, it had been about eight o'clock. Now at about half past nine the pattern repeated itself. I tried mightily to love her into a peaceful sleep. Intermittently I succeeded. Each time she nodded off, my legs ached enough that I tried to filch a break and a smoke in my favorite chair. Each time she erupted. Each time I gave in and walked her more. I put the TV on and watched some sporting event in snatches as I circled the first floor. I was dismayed at myself to think I was decadent enough to be cooing and baby-talking and assuring this puppy that I would take care of her, that she was safe, that if she insisted I'd take her back to Nolan Pazin in Athens in the morning and demand that he take her back so she could be reunited with her mother, Tara, and her siblings.

This had gone on for nearly two hours. Then at ten o'clock in exasperation I called my friend Bill Contardi in Manhattan. Bill has always been one of the most sensible and kind human beings I've ever been privileged to know. He laughed at me long and hard as soon as I explained the situation, but once he'd got it out of his system, he was all concern. He told me, "Don't be rash. Think of what a great companion she'll make." At the moment this was about as logical as whispering to Lenin in October 1917 to throw up his career as a subversive to turn venture capitalist. I couldn't imagine this crazy creature as good company.

Still, I knew Bill was touched by a placid wisdom about almost everything. "Give it two days," he counseled. I thought, *In two days Lynn will be here and she'll start knitting this puppy a blanket or a sweater or some damn equally sentimental and absurd thing.* But I said nothing. Dutchess, as I spoke to Bill on the phone, seemed to subside. A hint of lethargy was coming over her, I thought, hopefully. I figured at eleven at night she was bound to pass out with exhaustion from yelling her head off for the six straight hours I'd "owned" her. That verb was reminding me of slavery, and cruelty, and separating a tender creature from her mother at this brutally premature juncture in her life.

I actually heard myself laughing with Bill on the phone as he signed off to go to bed. I thought he'd be right. In an hour or two this cute little thing would keel over in her crate and I'd trek up to bed and cut some serious Zs.

In AA they warn you not to have expectations and not to entertain assumptions because they deliquesce into resentments as soon as reality melts their gold plating and reveals the heavy lead underneath.

It was a little after eleven at night on Tuesday. For years I had been in the habit of calling my friend Charlie McDade late at night to check on things and chew the fat and see how his writing was going. At this point he had published two novels and reams of poetry in the little mags and was teaching writing in a prison in Rockland County.

He had, because of a chronic predisposition toward clinical depression, a too-quick negative view of things, much like me too often, I'm afraid. When I told him how exhausted I was with the puppy, and how I feared I'd never have a quiet moment to write in again, and how I had offered to return the puppy, keep the cash, he said, "Get rid of it or you'll be in love with it before you know it. Take it back tomorrow." Charlie's advice was often good. He was brilliant and talented and deeply insightful about people. Yet somehow I kept thinking of what Bill Contardi had said. Especially the line about Dutchess eventually being "a great companion."

I remember thinking: Lynn was due into the Hudson train station at about ten-thirty Thursday night. That was less than two days away. I could endure two days of anything, I figured. I had no idea what lay ahead in that seemingly short span of time. In that interval Dutchess would grant me merely a smattering of catnaps as I stretched out exhausted on the living room couch with her perched on my chest asleep until she realized I was asleep too and loosed a primal screaming fit accompanied by frenzied scratching.

But it didn't matter because, as Charlie McDade had warned me, if I didn't "get rid of it immediately," I would be in love with "it" by morning.

By the time, a few hours later, I staggered around the yard behind her in the gray predawn no soothsayer had ever been more on target.

I was deeply in love with her before the sun was fully up.

CHAPTER EIGHT

Time lost all differentiation. There was no proper night, no usual morning, no languid afternoon, no restful evening of reading or watching a little TV. Of course there was no writing. In fact instantly Dutchess had developed an antipathy to computers. It may have happened when I took her into my study with the thing turned on within hours of bringing her to her new home. Lynn later theorized that maybe computers emitted a low-pitched hum only dogs could hear and this hum blew all of Dutchie's circuits. I think it may have been more basic than that. All her life she associated computers with Lynn or me being too occupied to play with her. No creature ever liked to play more than Dutchess did. For sure: She would not stay in a room with a computer on. She wouldn't have it. She was strong willed for a girl of infinite kindness and gentleness, for a girl who simply could not get enough affection.

Once she set her cap against computers she never wavered, let alone relented.

Within months of her arrival she fell into a pattern where she came up into my study every afternoon no more than fifteen minutes either side of four-thirty, and earlier in dead winter to allow for the shortened daylight. I would hear her padding up the stairs, and into the room she would come. Directly she marched to my office chair and clamped her teeth on my wrist or forearm until I turned the computer off and took her for our ritualistic walk. Of course, six months a year this walk led directly down to the waterfront dock of our neighbors Jimmy and Chris Warren. There she would put on her Esther Williams show for half an hour. In cold weather we walked up Riverside Avenue to the cemetery and walked through the cemetery to the back and then circled home along the edge of a small wood that led to a small plowed field beside our backyard. The whole walk covered a little over a mile. She insisted on it or the swim, weather permitting, no excuses accepted. I say "weather permitting" because she could not tolerate falling rain or snow pelting her.

What passed for our first night spent together was more of what I already described. I expected she'd calm down. She never did. I walked her in my arms throughout the first floor of the house. She took naps that way, in my arms. As soon as I attempted to join her in a little sleep, whether

I flopped into my special chair or stretched out on the couch, she ignited within minutes. Then it was back to cooing and cajoling her. I had paid attention to what Nolan Pazin told me about house-training her, so every hour or so I took her out into the backyard and crouched beside her or stood over her having a cigarette while I hoped she did her business.

Surprisingly to me, she caught on to this routine and started to relieve herself each time we went into the yard, probably as much from nerves as from any sense of it being the appropriate thing to do, the purpose of our outing. Nolan had told me dogs were very clean animals and detested to eliminate where they lived. He told me she would quickly learn not to relieve herself indoors, especially in her crate. He had told me specifically to take her each trip to the yard to the exact same spot. This I did. The spot was at the base of a wild silver maple that stood to the side of Lynn's studio. Lynn had ringed the base of this tree with fieldstones and planted a little flower bed inside. I would plunk Dutchie down beside it and wait patiently, glancing up at the stars and foolishly puffing away on yet another cigarette, looking for a little nicotine rush to counter my growing tiredness.

After five or ten minutes I'd carry her back inside, each time hoping this was the trip when she'd go into her crate, relax, and fall asleep. That was a pipe dream and dawn found us in the yard greeting my neighbors Lois Cameron and Janet Gerrain, who took a constitutional at daybreak each day. Of course they thought Dutchess was adorable, but by then so did I.

When I called Charlie McDade a few hours later to update him on where things stood, he laughed at me for keeping "it" and gloated a bit that I had, just as he'd predicted, fallen in love with "it." I laughed back at him and told him it didn't matter: She was too wonderful, and, what was really the key, I understood exactly how she felt, alone and afraid in a world she never made. My mother and father had never tired of telling me what a loud baby I was, how I cried half the night and kept the whole household up, how I was ever seeking attention, how, even as an infant, they couldn't "get me to go down," as they referred to an infant falling asleep at night. I related my condition then to Dutchess's condition now. My empathy with her was one-to-one solid; we were in complete harmony. Even to this day I am not good at going to sleep. I have the DNA of a raccoon, and love to read and write till the wee hours or, near the summer solstice, right through to daybreak. So what Dutchess was putting me through was touching me in profound ways. She was somewhat doing primal therapy for me by proxy, screaming her head off for both of us.

All during the daylight hours that next day I cozened to her every wish. It was personal now. I was going to calm her, hell or high water. I was going to convince her that I would care for her, that she would be safe with me, that I would love her to bits. In AA they had a saying that I arrogantly smirked at quite a bit: "We'll love you till you love yourself." Every time they would say it I would mentally cringe. It struck me as the worst sort of empty pablum: touchy-feely New Age vacuity at its apex. I wasn't having any of it from fellow AAs, yet here I was radiating the selfsame thing at Dutchess, aged seven weeks. I had no clue at the time, but I think in retrospect that I was relating not only at the conscious level to Dutchie's ontological panic but at the unconscious level also. I saw her panic as an infant as my panic as an infant, but I also must have seen it at the back of my mind as the panic, the nerve dance, that made me reach for my boozy tranquilizer.

At that point, in April 1994, I had been going to AA for only a few years. I was really only "of" AA and not properly "in" AA, since I would periodically conclude it was balderdash and take myself for a little toot that too often, and increasingly, would amount to a big bender lasting a few days. I had not yet heard the recommendation often made in AA that someone struggling for sustained sobriety should get a living organism, a pet or at least a plant, and take care of it. Dutchess would more than fill the bill here, but, as I say, I was oblivious of it at the time and, as I stated earlier, I was bent on humoring Lynn to get her off my back about what, in my delusional moments, I trivialized as my "high-spiritedness."

So that first day together passed with me catering to Dutchie, walking her around the first floor, petting her, cooing to her, cuddling her. Then we'd make the house-training run to the silver maple beside Lynn's studio and back. I marveled that Dutchie was catching on and doing her business on these junkets to the backyard. Whenever I sat in my club chair or stretched out on the couch, she would erupt into squeals and screams, but it was taking her longer and longer to do so, and I was catching little catnaps as her intervals of sleep between eruptions grew longer. She was settling in, gradually, grudgingly, but she was settling in. I must have snatched ten or fifteen minutes of sleep a few times before she realized I too was asleep and let loose her ire, waking me. Instead of being mad upon being roused so roughly I would go into overdrive with an affection assault.

Completely eccentric by now, completely crackers about this puppy, I was developing a language with her that would be all our own. "No, no, she's okay. She's Uncle Eddie's girlfriend and I love her so much. I love, love, love Miss Dutchie." I didn't know what else to call myself when addressing her, so I called myself what my nieces and nephews call me. Oddly, I felt outside myself and was laughing at myself, separated from my usual self, as though I were having another psychotic break with reality or having an out-of-body as well as an out-of-mind experience, yet I felt integrated, centered, whole. Mentally schizoid I was somehow emotionally unified.

Every time I lit a cigarette, Dutchess would crouch at my feet and raise hell. She obviously hated the cigarette for taking attention away from her, just as she hated the computer for the same reason, but she seemed also to detest the fumes and the smell and the smoky fog of this deadly habit. I have been in psychotherapy for over thirty-four years as I write this, and I have coined that neologism for my psychiatrist I mentioned earlier, *consciopath*. I am guilty at the drop of a peccadillo. This is no doubt the product of Catholic school for thirteen years in the fifties and early sixties, taught by nuns imported from Ireland for the purpose and by neurotic and maladjusted priests. That, capped off by my parents being convinced, especially my father, that child rearing in our house should roughly resemble boot camp at Parris Island, replete with heaps of corporal punishment, made me think early on that I was a repository of sin and iniquitous longings. At both home and school I was assured I was "up to no good" even when I wasn't doing anything at all.

So when Dutchie crouched like an angry lioness at my

feet as I puffed away on a cigarette it made me feel mega-guilt. I already detested myself, as a former athlete, for smoking, but to have a puppy emphasize the unaccept-ability of this vile habit brought home to me hard how repulsive it truly was. Like alcohol, nicotine, its sidekick addiction, acts on your brain like a vise as well, squeezing out self-esteem as you indulge it to your own demise, tightening your own suicidal bind on yourself. I wanted to quit smoking in my saner moments as much as I wanted to quit drinking, but my defiance of the helpful precepts of the AA program closed me off from attaining these goals. I had once quit both deadly habits for five years in my early thirties with the help of a psychotherapist, but now in my late forties the flywheel of my willpower kept slipping its gears and I was going nowhere fast when it came to shuck-ing these twin addictions.

My pathological embrace of guilt as a stimulant could be funny. Years later I would convulse an AA meeting of mostly women by telling them how my mother had threat-ened to take me to an ophthalmologist if I did not stop blinking compulsively. I could not tell her at about age ten that I kept picturing women in my mind's eye without their clothes. This was a mortal sin, the nuns had assured me, calling it "indulging impure thoughts," and my older brother, who would later spend five years in the seminary, had recommended that I try to blink such impure thoughts away. It was a losing battle. The thoughts remained but eventually I didn't do this blinking around my mom, though my Oedipal urge with her was massive, and I kept picturing her in the altogether, but this lunacy—the blinking, not the visualizing—did subside with age.

The same sort of thing had happened to me with the nuns ranting about touching yourself in the bath. I matured late and had no idea in seventh grade what they were talking about, but in my devout aspirations I tried to bathe and scrub clean without touching myself other than with a washcloth. I had no inkling that their euphemism of touching oneself referred to autoeroticism. I thought any touching, flesh on flesh, of your body, which they assured us was a "temple of the Holy Ghost," was verboten. Hence the washcloth buffeted my flesh when I bathed though the elimination of flogging the bishop was the object of this dictum. I was even more confused at an even younger age when the nuns would roar at us that we should never touch our "organ." I had no idea what they were referring to and thought everyone else had been born with a musical instrument on them that I had somehow not received, since I could find no evidence of one when I was naked in the tub.

The Catholic Church got you coming and going. In high school we learned that you could achieve a hat trick, so to speak, by getting a girl pregnant out of wedlock, the first mortal sin; if you had tried to prevent conception by using a condom when commissioning this act, a form of birth control, you had committed the second mortal sin; and, should the condom have broken and pregnancy resulted, if you had planned ahead for this possibility and determined to get the girl an abortion, you hit the trifecta and committed the third mortal sin. If you thought about all of this, and then the girl changed her mind about everything and refused to play hide the salami with you, you were still thrice guilty if you had contemplated all three eventualities, known all three were mortal sins, and consented in your mind to go ahead and commit them anyway, even though in reality the girl's change of mind meant you were jilted by your potential partner and deprived of the sinful but pleasurable payoff. When it came to sin nothing was a moot point. Fully contemplating sins and setting your cap to commit them was just as bad as actually committing them. You were Hell-bound no matter whether you got your jollies in or not.

Often in Catholic school I was walloped on the head out of the blue by a nun or priest, and when I asked what I had done, the nun or priest would say, "It's not what you did. It's what you're thinking of doing." I point this out to illustrate how easy it is to make me feel guilty, and to show how effective Dutchie's revulsion at my cigarette smoking made me feel intensely guilty, even on the first full day we ever spent together. But Dutchie's disdain was intensified by my own disgust. I really did loathe myself for smoking and wanted, very fervently, to quit. I wanted to get back to training hard as a runner and increase my wind to the high levels I had attained during my five-year hiatus from booze and cigs in my early thirties when I ran two marathons two weeks apart in a shade over three hours each.

That Wednesday, though sleep deprived, I was proud of myself. I lost my temper only once with Dutchess on our first full day together. Around eleven o'clock that night, exhausted but exhilarated by her company, I became aware I smelled from her decorating me occasionally for the past thirty hours. I was also sweaty from walking her constantly. I decided I badly needed a shower. But I wasn't going to be stupid about it. I took her upstairs to the bathroom with me. I wasn't going to be stupid and leave her all alone downstairs. All went well. Until I stepped into the shower and pulled the shower curtain to, shutting us off from each other. She went loopy, completely critical. I scrubbed maniacally fast but she laid siege to the curtain. She was stretching as high as she could against the side of the tub and smacking hard at the shower curtain as she sent up a death curdle of a scream. I kept hollering reassurances to her.

None worked. I quickly lost my temper and pushed the shower curtain back, jumped out of the tub dripping water, snatched her up in both hands, raised her as high overhead as I could reach, and shouted to her, above her squealing, "You're Uncle Eddie's girlfriend. Nothing bad is ever going to happen to you, understand!"

I kept that promise to her until fifteen minutes before six o'clock on the evening of June 9, 2006 when Dr. Bill Perkins entered the number one treatment room at the New Baltimore Animal Hospital with a hypodermic needle filled with barbiturates for Dutchess and I almost started shouting and then, three minutes later, nearly fainted when my girlfriend's heart stopped.

PART TWO

It is simply that, having once found the intensity of art,
nothing else that can happen in life can ever again seem
as important as the creative process.

—F. SCOTT FITZGERALD,
Letter to H. L. Mencken

CHAPTER NINE

Yesterday Lynn returned from one of her ritualistic leafing excursions in the Catskills and reported that she'd broken down crying at a rest stop she used to frequent when Dutchie accompanied her on her trips. I never go on these leafing jaunts but this particular rest stop has a mountain stream behind it and Dutchie loved to jump into the water and swim there. What set Lynn off was the arrival of a woman with two goldens. The woman asked Lynn why she started crying and Lynn explained. Then the woman asked if Lynn thought it would be okay for her dogs to go into the stream and Lynn nodded and watched the two retrievers take a dip. The woman told Lynn the only solution to her grief was to get another dog. "People tell you they could never go through losing a dog again, but it's worse to deprive yourself of one. Dogs are too wonderful," the woman said.

Lynn never got the woman's name. Probably the woman is right but it's hard to focus on getting a new dog. When Lynn got back to the house she asked me when we would scatter Dutchie's ashes and I dodged answering her. Writing this book with Dutchie's ashes downstairs in that tan canister with the blue flowers painted on it somehow spurs me on. Clearly Lynn and I are as neurotic as two exposed ganglia but I want to finish this short book with Dutchie's ashes still on the sideboard in the dining room. There's no explaining this. It's loony. As I write this paragraph it's four months to the day since Dutchie died.

I've just had an interruption of a month from writing this book. I had to do work for my literary agency and I also went to Philadelphia to visit my mother. I hadn't seen her in over six months. It marked the first time I visited her without Dutchie. My mom was close to Dutchie. After my father's massive stroke and subsequent cranial operation in 1994 I used to drive down during the week and ferry my mom to a suburban hospital to visit him each weekday, though he was only occasionally coherent and had mostly lost the ability to speak. Dutchie was a puppy then and she came with me. My mother had never been fond of dogs, in fact she called them "beasts," but she bonded with Dutchess.

Every morning when I awoke on the second floor of our three-story row house in Fairmount I would hear my mother down in the kitchen chattering away to Dutchie. Everyone thinks their dog is the brightest ever, the way people all brag about their kid's intelligence, but Dutchess did have a way of looking and listening that encouraged even strangers to talk to her. She could achieve absolute and exclusive focus on the person she was with. As any great actor can tell you, that's the secret to charm. Only Dutchie, at all times, was sincere. Whoever she was with enchanted her. She took that Stephen Stills line literally, "If you can't be with the one you love, love the one you're with."

The old neighborhood is so gentrified these days that I roar with laughter on the inside the whole time I'm there. On my last visit good old Fairmount was playing host to what was called the "Fairmount Art Crawl." All the great old bars are now chichi restaurants and bistros. McMenamin's is now the London, Patsy's is Rembrandt's, Milt's is Bridgid's, Eddie's is the Bishop's Collar, and Magee's, which my family ran as a speakeasy during Prohibition, is the Aspen Tavern. For what was dubbed the Art Crawl each establishment hung the work of a featured artist or two, and people were encouraged, via a cute map, to stroll from one "pub" to the next and take in all this artwork and maybe even buy a piece. These days Fairmount even sports a good used bookstore called Bookhaven, plus sidewalk cafés, a framing shop, upscale brick oven pizza joints, and, no kidding, a cybercafé on Fairmount Avenue across from the old Eastern State Penitentiary, no longer in use as a prison but a tourist attraction these days with Al Capone's old cell the biggest draw, featuring as it does an easy chair, an Oriental rug, a fancy lamp, and an old cathedral radio on which Al used to listen to Caruso belt out *belle canto* in Scarface's favorite operas. This cybercafé across the street is called, cleverly enough, Mug Shots. It even shows foreign films.

One night I passed there on my way to an AA meeting at the Fairmount Brewerytown Clubhouse, also opposite the old prison but one block farther down, and a sign in the window announced: TONIGHT'S SHOWING: *GRAND ILLUSION*, 7:30, DISCUSSION TO FOLLOW. The warfare in Fairmount, back in the pregentrification days, unlike Renoir's take on world conflict in his classic movie, used to feature guys tumbling out of these now dandified "pubs" when they were still shot-and-a-beer joints and brawling on the sidewalk till the "red car" arrived and the cops hauled the bloodied combatants off to the Ninth Precinct, down on Callowhill Street. One day on my latest visit I stepped out of my mom's house on Brown Street and there at the curb, top down, sat a canary-yellow Ferrari, black leather interior, ready to be stolen but no thieves abounded, not like the old days. I chuckled and grinned over this thought for several minutes.

. . .

To my shame I once took Dutchie to the only shot-and-a-beer joint left in Fairmount, Krupa's, one block up Brown Street from my mom's house. It was the fall of 1994 when my dad was so bad and his death seemed imminent. I had spent two overnights in the hospital sitting in his room so he wouldn't die alone. It left me spooky. By then I had already started to attend AA meetings but I was still a backslider, a "multiple relapser" as a woman once dubbed me. It took me those seven erratic years to really get a grip on the program. Till then I accumulated time but lost it as I went in and out of abstinence. I abhor AA jargon but when I took Dutchie to Krupa's I had "gone out," I was on what they call a "slip." In Fairmountese I simply "went drinking." Fairmounters use this phrase as other people use the expressions "went fishing" or "went shopping" or "went on vacation." It's quite an activity, "going drinking." You might not come back. At the end of my drinking, as a matter of fact, I almost didn't.

But I should never have taken Dutchie to Krupa's. A lady like her was out of place in a boisterous blue-collar bar like that. She later came to recoil from me whenever I had taken anything to drink. She shunned me. It hurt me. It made me think. She was acting just like my wife, Lynn. There was a message in it. Whenever men, and especially women, in AA bewail their drunken negligence toward their children, I understand it through this one incident with Dutchie, taking her to a bar when she was just a puppy. It pierces my conscience still that I did something that dumb and thoughtless with her. I should just have left her at home with my mom. Seeing Krupa's on my most recent visit, seeing all the yuppie watering holes in Fairmount, the rehabbed boîtes now bright and chic, I thought of those first visits with Dutchie to Philly when she was only months old. I flashed back on a mental picture of her crouched on the tile floor at the foot of my barstool in Krupa's, obviously uncomfortable, and anger at my foolishness in taking her there racked me top to bottom, yet again. When you finally get sober you ask yourself time and again what took you so long to finally get it.

Back then Dutchie seduced my whole family, she had such a winning personality, and all my nieces and nephews would vie for her attention. When Lynn and I had to go away to London on business, they would take turns minding her. She became the family dog, and I have a family the size of those procreators in the early chapters of the Bible, so she really got passed around a lot and became, within the family, rock-star famous. My feelings about her were always obvious to everyone. Even in his infirmity, my father, in one of his coherent moments, flashed his wit, and his contempt for me, by remarking to my siblings that, "Eddie thinks he's going to teach that dog to play the violin."

All during my recent visit with my mother, who had survived a bout with breast cancer the previous year, the absence of Dutchie was for me the elephant in the room, never mentioned. Under no circumstances would my mom bring up Dutchie's loss, dote on her though she had. My mom is as hard as titanium and as resistant to things sticking to her as Teflon. She says, "Life is just one damn thing after the other," and rolls with every punch. I should learn from that, but, then again, I'm haunted by time passing and a sense of loss and am morbidly pervious. When I was young I was thanatophobic and, reckless with drink, sometimes, though unaware of this, I acted as though I wanted to get death over and done with. I drove cars often under the influence at very high speed and with extreme recklessness, even drag racing on city streets. Another time, when a black kid, a member of a North Philly gang known as the LTs, held a saw-offed shotgun on my chest in a schoolyard gang showdown in Swampoodle, I did not panic or negotiate though, realizing this was probably curtains, I do remember thinking, *I'll never see my mom again.* That would have been my last thought had he pulled the trigger. This fact lets the Freudians know where my mother stood with me at the time, but it also shows, since I didn't mouth off to this psychotic, that I probably *did* want to live more than I wanted to die.

From early on, alcohol had associations for me of disrespect for life, my own and those of others. As I stepped out of the shower dripping and naked that second night I spent with Dutchie and held her aloft in order to get through to her that with me she'd be safe, that I'd take care of her always, I had no idea that she was about to cure me of the psychosis that underpinned this malady.

CHAPTER TEN

Dutchess kept me up all night that second night too. After my shower I thought for sure she would, like a cried-out infant, collapse exhausted into a deep sleep. Wrong yet again. She continued to nap against my chest as I sat watching television in the living room or reading, but the minute I attempted to put her back in her crate she erupted into paroxysms of squealing and barking. Whenever I fed her I had brief moments of peace, and I started giving her puppy biscuits for little respites of silence except for her munching. Once or twice I assumed I was being clever by petting her as she curled on the floor of her crate, but as soon as I thought she was sound asleep and went upstairs and got into bed she would let loose again and I'd have to hurry downstairs and comfort her. She screamed as though she were being butchered or tortured.

There was no possibility of my ignoring her long enough

that she would cease and desist and subside into sleep. I know because I tried. The longest I ever made it with the ignoring-her bit was about ten minutes. Her pain was jagged with urgency and I couldn't stand listening to it. A few times during that night I managed to stretch out on the couch with her asleep on my chest, but I was only able to nod off myself for a few minutes before she exploded the instant she figured out I was asleep and she was alone, unguarded. She must have intuited this sleeping of mine by my breathing turning shallow as my chest rose not quite as far with each new breath. It was my first lesson in how sensitive Miss Dutchie was to her surroundings and to other living organisms.

For over a dozen years this would continue to startle and astonish me. She had extrasensory perception, she was preternaturally psychic. Dog lovers of course had known this for centuries. Once or twice a few of them had mentioned it to me. Skeptic that I was, I ascribed it immediately to their nerdy weirdness and credited it not one iota. A few times during that second night I took her out into the backyard in total darkness to the same spot where she could relieve herself, house-training her as Nolan Pazin had told me to. I foolishly assumed that going to the bathroom one last time so late at night would signal to her, via ritual, that we should both retire until morning. This never happened.

Miss Dutchie newly arrived.
April 1994.

Miss Dutchie and me.
April 1994.

Miss Dutchie and her dad, Tar. April 1994.

Our new house guest. April 1994.

Poaching lilacs. April 1994.

Miss Dutchie and Lynn.
April 1994.

Teething on a tennis ball. April 1994

A man and his dog after a rousing game of tug-of-war. April 1994.

Miss Dutchie looking like a bear cub. April 1994.

Already the tug-of-war expert. Spring 1994.

Miss Dutchie settled in quickly. Spring 1994.

Being upbraided for breaking the rules. Spring 1994.

In her favorite perch,
five or six months old.
Summer 1994.

Miss Dutchie, newly
caught after a chase
around the yard.
Summer 1994.

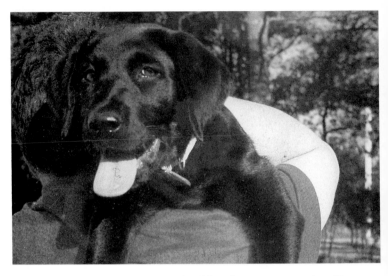

She loved to hitch rides on my shoulder, five or six months old.
Summer 1994.

Miss Dutchie in her breakfast-nook den with Monkey Man. 1998—1999.

Daybreak found us back in the yard, me hovering over her as she scooted around a little, exploring what would become her domain. Insomnia was nothing new for me to cope with; routinely from my twenties to my forties I could go as much as two days without proper sleep, yet I had never endured it to chaperone an animal. This annoyed me a bit but was outweighed by my irritated fascination with how wonderful she was. I could only have intuited this quality of hers for she hadn't demonstrated it yet. She was still all neediness, all egocentricity, all me, me, me; but I somehow felt her greatness of spirit nevertheless, by a kind of osmosis, I think now, looking back. My neighbors Janet Gerrain and Lois Cameron strolled by the front of our house and waved to me. They were, as always, taking their morning constitutional at dawn, like Harry Truman. Grinning and shouting, they wished me good luck with the puppy. It must have amused Lois especially that I had chosen a black Lab because Lois and her husband, Pete, had owned Suzie, the black Lab I had had so much fun jogging with and playing fetch-the-stick with on the riverbanks of the Hudson back when I worked full-time in the city and came to the country only on weekends.

I grinned back at them and shrugged, dragging foolishly on a cigarette while standing over my little fur ball, worrying when I would get back to writing my novel, the most important assignment in life I had ever given myself, or so I thought, and I said to myself, *Here I am frittering time away on this dog for Lynn instead of turning out pages. What a phony am I.* Knowing I had already fallen in love with Dutchess I nevertheless in my exhaustion blamed her time-consuming and novel-writing-wrecking distraction on Lynn. I needed a scapegoat for what I felt happening here, my feelings for something other than my literary ambition coming to the fore, eclipsing my ego. Lynn had served this scapegoat purpose handily for me in the past, as I had for her, and I saw no reason now to break the habit of a lifetime. Suffer shame as a child, assign blame as an adult. It's as simple as that.

The rest of that day is one big blur. I know I received phone calls to check up on me from the friends I'd called the day before. Ruth Leonard called and later Bill Contardi called. Finally Charlie McDade called and, as I mentioned, rebuked me, gloatingly, for not taking his advice. "I told you to get rid of it before you fell in love with it, idiot. I told you what would happen." He was irritated with me because he knew how dead set I was on completing my novel and he rightfully felt that I'd compromised myself with an extraneous impediment. I told him I had tried to give "her" (I didn't like him calling her "it") back to the breeder but that I was glad I hadn't succeeded. I was rubbery with exhaustion, I told him, but I was fascinated with her. The only thing that was really getting on my nerves was her habit of crouching at my feet as I smoked in my chair and snapping barks at me with each puff I took.

This was doubly irritating because my conscience also twitched and screeched at me with every drag I took. So now I was bombarded with disapproval signals in stereo. I hated myself for smoking. I had grown up admonished many times that athletes neither smoked nor drank. Since I played all three major sports as a boy I considered myself an athlete in training, even in my midforties. But, ever the rebel, I had embraced both habits of smoking and drinking, and both had cost me dearly. Still, I persisted foolishly with smoking even as I attended AA meetings and, in the main, except for my "slips," abjured the brewed, fermented, or distilled byproducts of grape and grain.

What worried me the most was that my iron will had, apparently, reached the limits of its tensile strength. I couldn't stop smoking. I couldn't stop relapsing into the occasional bender of a few days' to a week's duration. Though well spaced, these benders worried me and baffled my psychiatrist. I had landed in psychotherapy in 1974 after my first serious nervous breakdown, and I had been in treatment ever since. At that point in 1994 that span totaled two decades and counting. I was the Irish cognate to Woody Allen, I castigated myself internally, never comfortable with the idea of needing the help of a psychiatrist in life, having internalized my parents' bromide to "stand on my own two feet."

Yet, by the time Dutchie showed up, for over a dozen years I hadn't had any recurrences of real psychic turmoil, certainly no breaks with reality. I had heard no voices in my head. My delusional system had lain fallow. This is not to say that all in my mental and emotional life was smooth sailing, but neither was I corkscrewing in turbulent seas of my own manufacture, babbling to myself in public or answering people aloud who weren't there, which had happened to me twice in my twenties. That's what was so disconcerting about my inability to call a complete halt to the self-destructive habits of smoking and drinking.

Back in 1979, upon being told by my first psychotherapist that I was a "potential alcoholic," I had taken such umbrage that I promptly quit drinking and, four months later, quit smoking. I vowed I would show him, and I did. I quit drinking and smoking "cold turkey," as the accusatory psychotherapist put it. He had urged me to join AA but I took up marathon running instead and swiftly became addicted to that, to its endorphin high, though I wasn't aware of this psychological transfer at the time. I thought I'd just embraced a health kick and reverted to the discipline and regime of the dedicated athlete, something I had pursued fervently until my late teens, when drinking first reared its ugly head and I started down the path that led to sporadic drunkenness and then, whenever I had lately taken that first drink, to craven addiction.

Foolishly, even after my addiction was becoming quite obvious even to me, I kept telling myself I could handle quitting my foolhardy behavior on my own terms, without being babysat or brainwashed, as I thought of it, by AA or any other faddish, New Age folderol. I would just quit again, gut it out cold turkey. This was fine in theory but in practice I couldn't pull it off a second time. When I had quit everything the first time I had lasted those lovely five years, though I had lots of mental ups and downs and turmoil throughout that dry period, including breakdowns. But now was different. I felt a strong undertow from alcohol pulling me under and sweeping my willpower away. It annoyed me that my first psychotherapist had told me this would inevitably be the case. He had lots of experience treating alcoholics, I later came to realize, and he knew cold the patterns creeping alcoholism always took. "In five or six years you'll drink again," he had told me, quite smugly I remember thinking at the time. I thought he had said this in total ignorance of just how strong and determined my willpower could be. All young alcoholics think this way.

Five years and four months later in a snug in the basement pub of the Cashel House in Ireland I asked my wife if she thought there'd be any harm in my having one Guinness. Reluctantly she agreed. I had always heard that Guinness didn't travel well, and ever since reading *The Ginger Man* back in college with its homage to Guinness's great selling line, "Guinness Is Good For You," I'd wanted to try a pint of this malty elixir on the Olde Sod, just like Sebastian Dangerfield. Needless to say it wasn't good for me.

As any addict or alcoholic will know, the one drink was okay, at first, and briefly; but, even more quickly, it led straight to disaster. Soon I was back getting loaded on beer, and then I took a job in a corporation with a devoutly alcoholic culture, though mentioning this is not intended to assign blame for my alcoholism to anyone but me. My problem is my problem. But this corporate culture was big on fine wines, superb champagnes, exotic single malts, and aged brandies. Soon there were heavy lunches and besotted sales conferences and celebratory dinners soaked in booze. For a while I was able to fight back. I was struggling to do what they call in AA "controlled drinking." It never works and it didn't work for me. I would abstain from alcohol for a few days straight but end up right back "on" it. My predilection grew, my habit hardened, my thirst morphed into a craving, I became an addict, an alcoholic.

But at first I didn't buy this puritanical assessment of myself completely. Even when I still worked as a publisher I went to AA meetings but remained aloof, skeptical. I gainsaid nearly everything the program suggested. Having grown up in Quaker-ridden Philadelphia with its draconian blue laws, I viewed AA as a do-gooder Protestant conspiracy against Catholics having fun. I saw it as a dream extension of Carrie Nation's mania and as a teetotal crusade by the Roundheads. I lumped it together in my mind with the simplistic pieties of the Salvation Army and Major Barbara. Since college I had embraced Camus's "I rebel: therefore, we exist," only I had given it an egotistical, alcoholic twist, with a nod to Descartes, and it came out "I rebel; therefore I am," a sure prescription for disaster. So naturally I wasn't of a mind to retire my schooner, shot glass, and snifter anytime soon for good and all, especially once I started enduring keen frustration with my novel writing.

So for seven years I backslid. From time to time, after shunning booze for months on end—or even, once, for a year and a month—I would always decide I wasn't having any of this teetotal abstemiousness and revert yet again to hooch. I'd fall off the wagon, as they used to say back in Fairmount. I'd abandon the water wagon for the flagon of firewater. That's how I managed through impenetrable hardheadedness to celebrate two one-year anniversaries in AA, having blown off thirteen months of abstinence back in the midnineties.

Strangely, though, on that first full day with Dutchess, I did not want to drink to escape the annoyance she was causing me. I was irritated that I wasn't at my computer working on my novel, but I needed to take care of her more than I needed to do anything else at the moment. The way she admitted her total neediness charmed me. The way she went with the reality of her emotional state intrigued me. All of my training in life had been the opposite. Stiff upper lip, stand on your own two feet, never let them see you cry, never follow the crowd, do your own thinking, all that sort of crud. Right then I knew I needed to nurture this loud little ball of fur until Lynn arrived and relieved me. I desperately needed to take care of her and to calm her, and I focused on this task, this responsibility, religiously.

CHAPTER ELEVEN

The Dutchie mnemonics are everywhere. Grief itself is fueled by mnemonics. Everything reminds you of your loss. Yesterday I flew to Williamsburg to meet with my client R. Cameron Cooke and his family. When Dutchie died Rick wrote me an e-mail in which he said to visualize her running through a meadow on fresh legs. So I wasn't surprised at lunch yesterday when Rick asked me with his unfailing sensitivity whether Lynn and I had decided to get another dog. Of course on some levels this is the obvious solution to our cosmic funk at losing Dutchie. But then Rick proved again the poet in him. He grinned, shook his head, chuckled, and said, "But it's like remarrying too soon."

Only other animal lovers understand this. Spontaneously these days Lynn and I ask people on the street if we can pet their dogs. There are even two young dogs in our apartment building, one a Lab, the other a golden. We play with them when we meet them in the lobby. An elevator ride with them is a treat. Yet we can't get another dog right now. It's nuts, I know. It's only a dog we lost, so the solution is obvious: Get another one. But there are people out there who can understand this bind we're in, this paralysis. Certainly in my drinking and pre-Dutchie days hearing or reading anything like this I would have sneered, roared with laughter, and snapped, under my breath, "Bourgeois assholes." The "Bourgeois" is some leftover luggage from my sixties' rage, four decades old and flamed out somewhat but still smoldering. Even that, my sixties' rage, Dutchie helped tamp down, almost dispel entirely, with an assist from the AA program and its tried and true tenets, at least as this rage led me to act out in ways deleterious to my health.

Grief can be as tenacious as clinical depression, even though the shrinks usually classify grief with clinical depression's weaker sister, reactive depression. This morning Lynn was downtown in Tribeca and needed some information from her appointment calendar since she had forgotten to take it with her. She called the apartment and I picked up the calendar and it flopped open to the first week in June. My eye fell on this note Lynn had written on Sunday, June 4: "Dutchie appears to be limping on front foot—I borrow some Rimadyl from Chris and give to

Dutchie." I immediately think: *Dutchie had five days to live.* My time-conscious mind does a quick calculation: 120 hours, that's all she had left.

That same Sunday of June 4, encumbered with the possibility of reporting for jury duty the next day, I had stayed in town to clean up work for my agency. Now I think: *Schmuck, that's how you squandered the opportunity to spend your last weekend with Miss Dutchie.* I tell you my guilt gland wouldn't fit in the space allotted to all four heads on Mount Rushmore. But Lynn's the same. She's told me time and again Chris Warren called that Sunday and she took Dutchie with Chris and her two yellow Labs, Alice and Jasmine, for a walk down to, of all things, the cemetery. Next day when Dutchie could no longer stand up Lynn said the walk had taxed poor Dutchie to the point of ruin—and, ultimately, death. I always comfort Lynn that Dutchie's life was over anyway, walk or no walk. I tell her Dutchie was worn out and that her spine had snapped, on top of the laryngeal paralysis that had caused her such horrible breathing problems for the previous six months. Lynn always cries and indicts herself anew. I understand this perfectly.

The second night with Dutchie passed pretty much like the first one, only she was a little quieter and seemed to grow accustomed to perching on my chest as I lounged on the sofa catching catnaps until she caught on that I was asleep and exploded in a new demand for center-of-the-known-universe attention. I liked her self-absorption. I liked her demands for touches and for intimacy, of a sort. For years Lynn had complained that I was cold. I was. I loved a good, rousing, Rolfing, aerobic sexual encounter but I wasn't too big on "cuddling," as Lynn put it. I didn't like to curl up on the sofa and watch a movie on TV. Relaxing is hard for me. Instead, as the movie unspooled on our TV, I liked to sit up in my club chair and parse the screenplay as I watched, sipping coffee, thinking how I would have written, cast, or shot the film differently.

For years as an editor at Warner Books I had covered Hollywood for novelizations and had read oodles of screenplays. I loved the form and took courses back then, in the early eighties, in playwriting at the 92nd Street Y, and then tried my hand at both forms, plays and screenplays. It taught me much more about form and narrative flow and structure, not to mention characterization and dialogue, than any course I'd ever taken in college. The same held true for years of reading short stories and novels without ever really understanding these elements of storytelling as plays and screenplays made them come alive for me. The fault lay in me, I'm sure, but reading short stories and novels hadn't taught me an iota about story and structure compared to studying plays and screenplays and then trying to write them.

I didn't know, that second night Dutchie and I spent together, that she was taking me to school on relationships, but she already was. She needed strokes, petting, cooing, and hard and constant eye contact. She really was an intelligent dog, and I noticed right away that she would focus on you fiercely, staring at you as you spoke to her, seeming to read your lips *and* your mind at one and the same time. I lay there stretched out on the sofa talking to her and doubting my sanity and my manhood, my standing as a no-nonsense prole and a hard-fisted liberal eschewing the accoutrements of bourgeois life. I wasn't going to be like those ditzy spoiled dames bedecked with bling who strolled in front of the 2601 apartment house across from the Philadelphia Museum of Art, babytalking to animals and acting simpleminded. I wasn't going to act like some eccentric vicar in his Kentish rose garden trimming buds and babbling to his bassett hound.

No, not me. I was going to do this nurturing number only until Lynn arrived. Then I'd offload the responsibility to her, the kindest and gentlest human being I'd ever met. I'd retreat from the emotional and maundering mosh pit and return to my rich interior life of stream of consciousness musings, autobiographical reminiscences and chronological calculations, splendid fantasies, and debilitating resentments and rages, and the not infrequent impulse to dismember somebody.

. . .

Dawn next morning found us right back in the driveway. Dutchie was starting to scurry about, proprietarily exploring her new fiefdom. I trailed behind her in my moccasins, puffing away on a cigarette, whose smoke she didn't seem to mind in the outdoors. As she kind of explored smacking the spalls of driveway gravel with her paw, I stood glassy-eyed behind her, wondering for the first time how I had become, within hours, a kind of nanny to a Labrador retriever puppy. Had I known then that a dozen years later I'd be playing Boswell to her Johnson I would have collapsed in outraged laughter at my own expense, at my own derangement. Or, worse, that I'd end up not just chronicling her life but eulogizing her. How would this ever stack up against my undergraduate enthusiasm in Mr. Hollis's poetry course for "Tintern Abbey" or "When Lilacs Last in the Dooryard Bloom'd"?

Standing there in the driveway I laughed at my crazy turn of mind and reveled in mocking myself. Then my reverie was shattered when I heard Lois Cameron and Janet Gerrain holler, "Good morning, Ed." They were smiling and laughing and starting up the driveway toward us. Dutchie scrambled toward them. She never met anybody she didn't like instantly. I hurried down the drive. As Lois stooped to pet her I shouted, "Careful, Lois, she's a biter." Lois and Janet looked at each other and grinned hard. By then I was at their side and flashed my right in-dex finger as evidence. Dutchess had used it as a teething toy. It was perforated with tiny holes like a thimble. The holes were red and raw. There were tiny patches of torn skin interspersed among the holes. Like all puppies Dutchie had teeth like needles and she plunged them into you every chance she got. As much as I already loved her I feared she might be feral. Lois and Janet pulled out of their hardy grin and Lois said, "Ed, all puppies bite. And you look like you desperately need some sleep. When was the last time you slept?"

"Monday night. Before I brought her home."

"That's crazy. You need to sleep."

"I can't. She panics when I leave her and go upstairs. She even panics when I fall asleep holding her."

"You've got to get some sleep."

"Lynn'll be here in a few hours and I'll sleep then. And I'm catching these forty-wink deals on the couch hold-ing her."

"Put her in the basement and get some sleep."

I could never put her in our "basement" because it was a cellar with exposed brick and stone walls and a cement floor, cracked, pitted, and, in places, often puddled with seeping groundwater. It could serve as a crypt in a tale by Edgar Allan Poe. It was damp and cobwebby, dirty and awful. I'd never put her there. Lois had a beautiful finished basement in the prettiest and most tasteful split-level ranch house I'd ever been in. She couldn't know what horrors she was suggesting to visit on Miss Dutchie. By now Janet and Lois were playing with Dutchess and she was responding joyously, already a little performer, a star. In Manhattan she would perfect this act, especially on Broadway and in Central Park, where her patented strut and amped-up grin induced people to stop and pet her and talk to her. But that morning Lois and Janet were the first "room" I'd see her work. She did it supremely well and they left giggling. I got Dutchie back in the house and the day passed in a pleasant haze of charged waiting for Lynn to arrive.

Finally that night the moment arrived for me to go fetch Lynn from the Hudson train station. Usually when she arrived from the city on Thursday nights after teaching at the School of Visual Arts on Tuesday and Thursday, with an off day on Wednesday, she was fairly well wiped out. I had to be especially careful this night to act normal. When I picked her up at the train station I didn't so much as mention that her birthday gift had arrived, the one I had told her a month earlier was out of stock. Oddly enough that evening Dutchie had subsided a bit. She would curl in her crate on the far side of the kitchen and sleep. I couldn't believe it.

This happened so late in the evening that I had no time

to catch a quick nap before heading out to get Lynn. Truth to tell, it didn't matter. I was too pumped up to sleep now. I was burning major adrenaline reserves and I was dying to see Lynn's reaction. Before I left the house I wrote on a piece of eight-by-eleven white bond paper: "Hello, Lynn, my name is Dutch and I'm your birthday present. I'm all yours."

I taped this piece of paper on the top of Dutchie's crate. Lynn had told me for years that her aunt had had a dog named Dutch when Lynn was growing up and that if she ever got a dog she would name the dog Dutch.

When I doused the lights in the kitchen to leave, Dutchie didn't make a peep.

I headed for the train station all jangled with nerves, all anticipation, yet counseling myself to be cool.

CHAPTER TWELVE

When we got back to the house I let Lynn go in first. I followed close behind and hit the kitchen light. Lynn later told me she immediately sensed a presence in the dark kitchen. Only fools doubt women's and artists' intuition, and she's both, so I'm sure she did. As soon as the light flooded the kitchen, Lynn did stop dead in her tracks and stare toward the far corner. Dutchie had heard us arrive and was standing in her crate—quietly, for a change— staring straight back at Lynn and wagging her tail. Lynn started to cry. When I think back on it I realize it was one of the best moments in our marriage, and we've had a lot of great moments. Oddly this one was even better than our simultaneous climax in our top-floor room at the Hotel Quai Voltaire in the summer of 1981 when the Bateau Mouche passing below on the Seine flashed its lights at precisely that moment and punctuated our lovemaking with an operatic burst of light, rendering that encounter positively Wagnerian in my overactive imagination.

Now the stillness in the kitchen was portentous. I could hear Lynn's silent weeping, though, standing behind her, I couldn't see the tears. Dutchie broke the tableau by scratching around the crate and climbing against the wire mesh with her forepaws, creating a small commotion.

"This is your present, honey, that was out of stock," I said.

Lynn laughed through her tears. Then she walked over and read the note hanging on the crate and cried a little harder.

"Get her out and meet her," I said, stooping down to open the little door. I took Dutchie into my hands and placed her in Lynn's arms. Wouldn't you know she was quiescent with Lynn? And continent? Lynn just rocked her in her arms.

"She wasn't old enough to be taken from her mother on your birthday," I said. "I can't believe she's this calm. For two days she's been raising Cain in here. I haven't been able to get a minute's peace, let alone any real sleep."

Lynn laughed and said, "She's so beautiful."

"We better get her out in the yard. I've been following instructions on how to house-train her."

We took her out to the spot beside the silver maple tree

to the side of Lynn's studio and Lynn watched her move around the yard for the first time. I had hit the floodlights on the back of the house and Dutchie was a little black spot moving around on the semidark lawn. When we went back in the house excitement reigned. Lynn forgot her usual exhaustion after two days of teaching college kids and I got such a charge at seeing their joy together that I felt a rush of energy as well. It took well over two hours for Lynn to feel tired enough that she had to go to bed, and I went right along with her, up the stairs and into bed, exhaustion having induced a set of sea legs in me. Dutchess, amazingly, went into her crate and curled up, totally quiet. I had by this time regaled Lynn with a blow-by-blow description of what Dutchess had been like on her first two days in her new house. We laughed hysterically. But then in bed the bottom fell out of me. I held Lynn briefly, then nodded off. But just as I did Lynn voiced the sentiment I had choked back for the whole afternoon that day.

"Honey, what have you done? How are we going to take care of her? Do you think we'll be able to? With our crazy schedules?"

"I don't know, but it's too late now. I'm in love with her."

"So am I."

"Go to sleep. Unless I miss my guess she's going to really cut loose at six o'clock."

Lynn rolled over and peppered my face with kisses but I simply passed out.

Movies condition us all. The next few days, even months, passed in a kaleidoscopic blur of delirious fun, like montage scenes spun in quick-time. Dutchie galvanized us, uplifted us, entertained us. I found my attention riveted on her and my depression banished because of her. In memory the whole time is like those great sequences in the old Max Sennett Keystone Kops films, where the motorcycles whirl in tandem out of a garage and chase old sedans in double-time, choreographed in controlled chaos, crisscrossing one another at intersections by nanoseconds, avoiding accidents. Or it's like those mad sequences in the ingenious Coen brothers' *Raising Arizona* where the toddler wheels through the ranch house, the parents in frantic pursuit. Sometimes the scenes are as tightly focused and as bird's-eye-view as the tracking shots in Kubrick's *The Shining* when the tricycle roars through the abandoned vacation lodge, rooms and doorways whipping past in redundant but exhilarating monotony. I guess this was because I couldn't get enough of being on Dutchie's level, literally. I spent time on the floor with her, I spent time on the lawn with her, I spent time sprawled on the couch with her crawling all over me. Her joie de vivre was infectious.

For weeks my production with the novel fell off. I would

work a little, but it wasn't effective. There were too many interruptions to check on Dutchie, and, truth to tell, there were too many interruptions where I just wanted to play with her. When Lynn was upstate with us, it was the same for her. Rituals developed quickly. Dutchie was devilish, and quick. Even as a puppy she was too fast for me to keep up with her. No sooner did we take her into the yard than she learned to scurry under the deck, one of the many funny things she did that Lynn and I reminisce about often. Whenever she went under the deck we couldn't get her out until she was good and ready to come out. Not that I didn't try. The ground clearance on the deck varies from about six to eight inches. I could fit no more under it than my arms, and to do this I would have to lie flat on the ground facing the deck, with the shrubs sticking me in the head and shoulders, always annoyingly and sometimes painfully.

Dutchie would see me and move out of reach. That's when I learned that dogs have a kind of laugh, at least Dutchie did. She would flash a high-powered grin and whip her tail in fast and furious semicircles. She would come close enough to my outstretched arms to tease me, brushing against my hands quickly. Lynn would be stooped down on her knees imploring Dutchie to come out from under there, but to no avail. For Dutchie it was a game, fun; there was nothing sadistic about her taunting, she simply wanted to prove she could outwit and dominate us. Some-times our neighbors would watch this sideshow to their almost limitless glee. Always Dutchie would relent when ready and come out, dirty and muddy on her legs and belly. But we did learn a way to lure her. Lynn, who knew dogs far better than I, took to fetching a dog biscuit from the kitchen and trapping Dutchie when she came near enough to eat it.

In those first weeks and months Lynn could not stand to be separated from her puppy. When she had to teach her college classes she would go down to the city and then return as quickly as possible. Except for going into the city to see my psychiatrist, I would stay in the country with Dutchie, working at my novel in a desultory fashion and falling harder and harder in love with "Lynn's puppy" with each passing day. Like Samuel Johnson or Gertrude Stein or Proust, I like to work at night and sleep till midday or slightly later. When Lynn was in the city and Dutchie was alone with me, she was having none of that. Down in the kitchen in her crate she would set up a racket in the morn-ing until she was old enough to climb the stairs and sleep beside our bed in her dog bed.

I mistakenly thought then that she would sleep in later. No such luck. Even though she would stay up late with me when I worked at night, she fell into the habit imme-diately of rising from her dog bed early and coming to my side of the bed and pouncing on my chest until I woke and started to rub her head vigorously. Then she would lick my face until I climbed out of bed and hurried downstairs with her. She would run to the back door and, as soon as I let her out, do her duty in the yard before turning heel and coming back into the kitchen, woofing and snorting as she ran directly to her bowl. I was expected in the short time she attended to her toilet in the yard to have filled the bowl brimful of breakfast. I knew my duty and tried never to disappoint her.

Driving her snout into the bowl she dispatched her breakfast in short order, came up grinning and twirling her tongue over her lips and chin, lest any morsel of food be lost, before snatching one of her favorite stuffed toys between her jaws and retreating into the dining room, where she expected me, a guy who likes to take at least two hours to warm up to the new day, to chase her around the table in pursuit of the toy, falling to my knees to crawl under the table and cut her off in her circuit of it, so we could have our tug-of-war for the toy, her clenched jaws pitted against my straining hands and arms. I usually managed to last ten minutes before my body screamed for caffeine and I quit and made my first of three or four pots of coffee for the day, mostly decaf but with a kicker of espresso thrown into the first pot of the day. After that first pot I always switched to decaffeinated to avoid acting like I had, as the Irish in Philly like to say, "St. Vitus's Dance." Dutchie, on the other hand, needed no stimulants at all. Life itself was heady enough stimulant for her. She leaped right into her new day, grateful for it and determined to make the most of it. She had no idea in doing so she exemplified two of the cornerstone tenets of AA.

Before long, in a good-hearted way, Lynn started to complain to me that Dutchess was my dog. Lynn was simply chiding me. There was no real dispute. But that is not to say that for the next dozen years Lynn and I wouldn't debate the matter. The truth, though, was simple: Dutchess was never so happy as she was when all three of us were together. When the three of us went for a walk, when the three of us went to the river for a swim, when the three of us traveled together in the car, she was happiest. This compulsion of Dutchie's to be one with us had comical aspects. One afternoon when Lynn was at the kitchen sink I turned her around and embraced her. Dutchie, somehow with her infallible instincts, sensed this. She rose from her dog bed in the breakfast nook, from which you cannot see the rest of the kitchen because of a partial wall, so she didn't see us, and came around the corner and over to us. As I hugged Lynn and she giggled because she had noticed Dutchess over my shoulder, Dutchie got semifrantic before rearing up on her hind legs and perching with her front paws on my forearm. Lynn and I started to laugh hysterically and ended up taking Dutchie to the river instead of going upstairs for a matinee.

This became a pattern: Whenever I embraced Lynn, Dutchie made it a threesome if she could. The same was true whenever Lynn would plop into my lap in my big club chair next to the fireplace. Even though Dutchie was usually in her lair in the kitchen, on her bed in the breakfast nook, something in Lynn's voice or giggle would tip her off, and into the living room she would scamper and jump up on Lynn and me, sending us into gales of laughter, especially when Dutchess would fall back onto the rug and rebound, with added spring in her legs, right back into our laps. Eighty-five pounds landing on you suddenly could jolt you, but her need to be included, to get in on the affection, was so loving, and so human, that the humor would cancel the discomfort.

As for those first few days with Miss Dutchie in residence, I remember that I had to go to the city the day after Lynn's introduction to her. It was tax time and I had tax business to take care of. In fact, rare for me, I would be slightly late by a day or two in filing that year. As soon as I drove out of our driveway I felt Dutchie's loss. It was like a kid being separated from his favorite new plaything on Christmas morning. When I reached the city I called from the apartment first thing to check on her. Lynn was giddy and immediately started telling me of all the mischief "the Dutchess," as I sometimes referred to her already, was getting into. On one of her duty runs she had disappeared under the deck and refused to come out despite Lynn's pleas. In fact, I remember now, that was the first time she pulled this trick, which of course she soon mastered and Lynn had to solve with the dog biscuit as a lure.

I remember what a warm and sunny April day that Friday was, because after Lynn assured me that our new girlfriend was back in the house safe and sound I strolled down Columbus Avenue missing every moment together with my two ladies and wondering what the future would hold. I once read that someone remarked that F. Scott Fitzgerald had a head full of time awareness. I think the remark alleged that his head was full of "clocks and calendars." Mine is like that as well, and this weird chronological obsession sometimes takes a morbid turn. Right there on Columbus Avenue in all that glorious spring sunshine I remembered someone telling me the average life expectancy of a Lab was twelve years. I then thought, *If that holds true, Dutchess will die in 2006.*

She did.

CHAPTER THIRTEEN

Relationships, if you're lucky, develop rhythms and rituals. Mine with Dutchie quickly did. I'm relieved to say that my production on the novel I was writing quickly reverted to form, but my writing schedule evolved to include the rhythms and rituals Dutchie injected into it. I am no more a morning person than the average jazz musician or, as I said earlier, Dr. Johnson, Marcel Proust, or Gertrude Stein. I mean to draw no comparisons in talent with these three heroes of mine, only to say that I hold no brief for Ben Franklin's American go-getterism. As far as I've always been concerned, fuck the early bird, fuck the worm, and, while I'm at it, fuck Ben Franklin, whose smarmy philosophy and ingrained hypocrisy is odious to me, always has been and always will be.

I'd rather read or write late into the night, till dawn even, than rise and shine to grub for money the way a hog snorts for truffles. A monumentally great professor I had in college, Ms. Flora Binder Jones, a native North Carolinian, told me once, "Competition with others is vulgar, Edward. Compete against yourself, against what you can do or make in life, regardless of what others may be up to." I took that advice to heart. All real artists do.

Dutchie was like that too, a kind of artist. She saw her work as relationships and her life as a quest for fun and affection. With this philosophy she infected me. From her initial panic and total neediness she settled into a pattern of giving affection and seeking fun. The more affection she gave, the more I gave in return. The more fun she sought, the more I provided in return. The delightful rhythms and rituals of our relationship resulted from that symbiosis between us. Now that she's gone I miss all of it almost as much as I'd miss breathing. Its loss is a kind of living death.

Of course as Dutchess aged my rituals with her changed. At first I couldn't get out of the house without her wanting to ride in the car with me. We had the Toyota Corolla hatchback then, and she would bound into the backseat with no trouble. The Corolla was low to the ground. Later when we had a Subaru Forester and it was higher off the ground she couldn't get into the backseat without help; toward the end, without lots of help. The same with leaping onto our bed for a nap. In the early years she did it with ease. Toward the end I had to pick her up and put her in. She always resented needing help. It hurt her sense of independence, and she was as fiercely independent as she was devotionally loyal, an oxymoronic combination that can't be beat. I've been twice lucky; Lynn's the same.

In the early years she also ran to the door whenever Lynn and I returned to the house or the apartment. Toward the end she didn't. She stayed in her dog bed and we had to go over to her and greet her. In the city and in the country she started to decline long walks. When she was a puppy she loved to meander through Central Park to the north end of the lake and then take an illegal swim while I sweated out the hundred-dollar fine if the Park Rangers caught us. Toward the end she would only walk along our block on West Eighty-sixth Street, no farther, always mooching biscuits off the doormen as she went. Broadway at two full blocks away was too distant for her to make the trip. So there went her Broadway strut. People are funny about older dogs, too. As she aged people were not as attracted to her. She handled her reduced status with dignity, the way she handled every decline and setback sent her way.

Lynn regretted all the slowing down with Dutchess every bit as much as I did. But there was a compensation for both of us. As Dutchess lost energy and mobility, she stepped up her outpouring of affection. She liked to be visited on her daybed and caressed and cuddled while being cooed to and rubbed down. Evolving in a relationship and compensating for slowed-down playfulness and ardor is yet another thing Dutchess demonstrated so well. She seemed not to fight life's realities at any level. In AA terms she accepted life on life's terms at all times. Throughout every stage of her life she regarded stress as a waste of time and worry as out of the question. That's ironic, since the novel I was working on then I had titled *Worry Later* after the great Thelonious Monk composition.

I certainly didn't know how to accept life on life's terms, or how to accommodate stress anymore, or what to do to contain or cancel worry. I was getting worn out with not connecting with myself on paper the way I wanted to. When my novel was turned down, it soon became clear to me that I would have to return to the book publishing business in some capacity. During the two years I had worked on my novel I had turned down a number of offers for good positions in the book business, but especially after my dad became fatally ill I redoubled my efforts to hammer and tong my novel into publishable shape so he could see it and hold it in his hands before he died, sappy as that ambition for him on my part might have been. He had endured a full cranial operation after his stroke and it left him a vegetable 98 percent of the time, so my efforts might well have been pointless and Sisyphean, but still I worked away feverishly on the novel.

Miss Dutchie jousting with me in the front yard.
Spring 1998–1999.

My two special ladies and me. Spring 1998–1999.

On our front yard. Spring 1998–1999.

On our front porch. Summer 1998–1999.

A happy threesome. Summer 1998–1999.

Dutchess and me at Riverside Park, Coxsackie, where she did her Esther Williams imitation fetching tennis balls from the Hudson. Fall 1998–1999.

Dutchess and Lynn in Riverside Park, with Coxsackie, the Hudson River, and fall foliage behind them. 1998–1999.

The three of us in the front yard of Lynn's mother's house, Middleburg, Pennsylvania. Fall 1998–1999.

The grand old lady in front
of the Christmas tree with
Monkey Man. 2004.

The older Dutchess tires easily, but still loves a belly rub after a game of fetch the tennis ball. Summer 2004.

Lynn tends her flower gardens with her devoted assistant. Summer 2004.

Miss Dutchie relaxes in the snow, something she loved to do. Winter 2005.

Although suffering from laryngeal paralysis and shortness of breath, Miss Dutchie still liked to fetch a tennis ball. Spring 2006.

A game old retriever, Dutchess still plays fetch the tennis ball. Spring 2006.

The last picture of Pennsylvania Dutchess, her special lilac bush visible behind her. She's resting in front of Lynn's studio. Spring 2006.

I have a hard Irish head but a soft Irish heart. The combination may account for my split personality. That's a layman's diagnosis for what may underpin my seven or eight nervous collapses that occurred from my late twenties to my early thirties. I really don't know and I really don't care. That stuff's academic now. With the help of my psychiatrist, I haven't had a mental meltdown for over a quarter century, and, certainly living the high-stress life I did, and compounding matters with generous dollops of alcohol, it's remarkable that I've come through, in the main, compos mentis.

When I was young and first arrived in New York City I fell in love with book publishing, especially with the people in it. That's not to say though for me it was an imaginary garden of delights all the time and didn't have, among all the wonderful people in it, a couple of Marianne Moore's real toads too. But to divert attention to them is to miss the majesty of most book people, the oddballs, the compulsive readers, the furtive poets manqué, the connoisseurs of prose in English, the dreamers, the polymaths, the media maniacs and the lusters after fame and immortality by proxy. So the prospect of returning to book publishing did not daunt me, or in any way disappoint me. When writer friends implored me to set up shop as an agent and represent them, I thought I'd like to give that a go. I wanted to try book publishing from the other side, gamekeeper turned poacher.

This change did entail surrendering one aspect of my brief bohemian idyll, writing away in the Catskills till the wee hours or till dawn. I hated to relinquish it. My friend the painter John Lees calls this "The Upside Down Schedule." Like Morandi, John likes to draw and paint in his studio at night, just the way I like to write and read late into the night. Being a literary agent meant I would have to change that. Ever since high school and especially college, when I started to go on this late night schedule, my father had railed at me to "get in step with the rest of the world and stop thinking you're so goddamned special." To say my father was profane is like saying Shakespeare was eloquent.

Of course, like me my dad ended up alcoholic; that is, like me, he ended up just like *his* father. That would be my grandfather, "Big Barney," who managed to be barred from all the taprooms in Brewerytown and Fairmount. Being banned from bars in North Philly is like being expelled from the NRA for being overly fond of ammunition. When they tell you in AA that alcoholism is a family disease, never doubt it. My mother's side of the family has some alcoholism in it too though she is not a drinker; but on another DNA scorecard, my mother's the one, the geneticists tell me, I got my dose of Type 2 diabetes from. My mom has it also, and her mother had it before her.

I didn't intend to go on a Senecan Amble here. I simply wanted to point out what I'd miss the most in giving up my artistic sojourn, writing a novel in the mountains. But I got fooled again, as so often in life I had been fooled before: I didn't realize that my lifestyle change would involve so much separation from Lynn and Dutchess. I imagined that I would be back in the book publishing business, but as an entrepreneur this time, not as a corporate cog, and that prospect thrilled me. I have done time in many corporations and I never experienced one that didn't fundamentally try to infantilize everyone in it except the guy or gal at the top. By becoming an agent and being my own boss I hoped to avoid this condition and experience more freedom of movement: with e-mail and cell phones and all the tools of modern communication, you can agent from the country as easily as from the city, I assumed wrongly. I ended up spending lots of time in the city, including many weekends, especially because I had to take on book doctoring, editing, ghostwriting and writing assignments, often with tight deadlines, to supplement my agency income. Also, by becoming an agent I imagined that I'd now be purely on the side of the writers as their advocate. That prospect pleased me as well. So I opened my agency in January 1996.

Another thing I didn't anticipate was that Lynn would soon, for economic reasons, have to give up her downtown studio in the city and retreat to her upstate studio most of the time. This setback stemmed from the drying up of the market for freelance book jacket and record album design. In doing so Lynn would have Miss Dutchie up there with her most of the time. I would be alone in the city without my two ladies, and, though I had no crystal ball to forewarn me, my moods would swing widely and darken ominously. For the following two years and one month I would have well-spaced "slips," and, afterward, my anger at myself, my self-loathing, my frustration and my loneliness, would escalate.

Being isolated in the city like that without really understanding the depth and power of the AA Fellowship was going to be a disaster for me, but I didn't know enough about alcoholism and myself to realize it then. I did realize I would miss writing away for hours each day. I would never give up trying to write well. But, above all else, I didn't realize how much I would miss Miss Pin, as I sometimes call my wife, based on a girlhood nickname she had because she was so tall and thin, and I also didn't realize how much I would miss the everlastingly joyful, irrepressibly playful Miss Dutchie.

CHAPTER FOURTEEN

Dutchie was two when I had to return to the city and commerce. She was at her peak of health, and fun and playfulness, completely in her prime. I would see her on most weekends and that's when the wild ritual started with my arrival on Fridays at the bus station in Kingston. Waiting for me to get off the bus she would grow frantic. This sometimes disconcerted some passengers who preceded me off the bus. They interpreted her lunging on her leash as aggression and not, correctly, as scarcely contained affection. When I would finally emerge from the bus, Lynn would hold her tight while she jumped up and put her paws on my shoulders as I stooped to say hello to her. Her tail would be whipping in a flashing semicircle and she would lick my face so hard that people would laugh and often ask to pet her. She would charm them before I could settle her down and get her to climb into the car and leave.

That's when she used to stand in the backseat and lean over the front seat and lick the side of my face as we drove back up the thruway and Lynn and I gently debated whose dog she really was. Of course the minute we hit our yard and she vanquished any rabbits or squirrels who'd invaded her space, the game was on, and I had to chase her vigorously for fifteen minutes circling the outside of Lynn's studio. I had run seriously for years, especially during that five-year spell when I had quit drinking and smoking on my own and taken up a rigorous physical training routine, so I was still in good enough shape to give Dutchie a real workout. All of this, after a week of work in the city, was more a tonic for me than it was for her.

My entire weekend would then be a slice of heaven with my "girls" on either side of me. The argument over whose dog she really was was moot. She was both of ours and she reveled in our walks and her river swims with Lynn and me together with her. The other great pattern we fell into during these years was the city visits Lynn and Dutchess would pay to me. Dutchess would visit me in the city whenever Lynn was in to teach, to meet other artists or gallery people, for museum visits or for business or doctors' appointments. Then I would find myself walking Dutchie on Broadway or through Central Park in midafternoon when the book business was on lunch break. She provided the greatest respite in the middle of the day I'd ever experienced.

At that time I was also peridiabetic, a medical condition not yet recognized. But after I ate I became so lethargic I needed a nap. Dutchess was a great napping partner. I would grab two dog biscuits from the carnival glass cookie jar on our kitchen shelf and, alert and reading signals like an Indian scout as always, Dutchess would catapult herself off the floor in the living room, even when she appeared to be sound asleep. The clack of the cookie jar lid would arouse her, and she'd follow me into the bedroom, leap onto the bed, devour her two biscuits, thrust her rump against my leg or side, and fall asleep with me. I envied her her ability to sleep on demand. The glucose rush would knock me out, which was welcome because since my early teens I'd had those major problems with insomnia I mentioned. Short of good sex a refreshing nap in the middle of the day is hard to beat. And Dutchie's company, as ever, relaxed me, especially her sighing and her ability to let go and sleep whenever she needed it. I was starting to learn all sorts of things from her. She seemed to know the secret to enjoying life.

Like most alcoholics I'm defiant and like most alcoholics I too easily dismiss what's good for me. So when I had my nearly seven-year in-and-out, up-and-down flirtation with "the program," as we adherents refer to the regime of

Alcoholics Anonymous, I resisted and rejected lots of its suggestions as nonsense. I thought they smacked of a general grinding dullard's abhorrence of life's pleasures. Lynn didn't see my drinking quite this way, and I drove her into Al-Anon. When she first told me she was attending these meetings, I blew my lid and threatened to divorce her for "falling into the hands of a cult and acting like a half-witted Moonie."

When we were young Lynn and I used to have flare-up arguments, which I loved because they never lasted long and were never really serious, and, here's the real reason, because we inevitably ended up resolving matters by turning into Kama Sutra gymnasts and banging each other legless. This fed my Stanley Kowalski misprision of myself but worked wonders for our stability as a couple. The trouble was I'd grown up in a house with my father roaring like a demon out of Hell, and Lynn's mother in their house had done a stunning imitation of a Tennessee Williams termagant, so our early-days arguments, fashioned on the wrong models, were more Edward Albee acerbic than *The Honeymooners* sweet, and involved raised voices. Dutchie's first lesson for us was, whenever Lynn or I raised our voice, which was rare now that we were older and more mature and settled, anger was unacceptable. She left the room instantly.

Dutchie brought this lesson in domestic harmony home sharply and very early. The very first summer she lived with us, in August 1994, Lynn and I left her in her crate in the apartment to attend Lynn's cousin's wedding in Madison, New Jersey. When we returned I opened the door on her crate and told her to come out. She didn't. She sulked near a far corner and refused to move. I then raised my voice and commanded her to come out, as a dog trainer had told me to do. I needed to take her for a duty run. She retreated farther into the end of the crate and wouldn't come out until I realized why she was sulking. I crawled into the crate on my hands and knees, in suit and tie, and apologized to her with rubs and hugs and kisses for our having been gone for six straight hours, and for then having the gall, when we finally did return, to raise my voice to her. She didn't relent easily, forgiving though she was on most matters. After about ten minutes of coaxing, me half in and half out of the crate, she finally did relent and came out into the living room.

This scenario convulsed Lynn no end. It was abjectly craven on my part to crawl into the crate but it set me to thinking and to questioning my own behavior in raising my voice to her when she was obviously hurt. It marked the first stage in a whole tutorial Dutchie set in motion that day, when she was only half a year old. Who was I to abandon a loving Labrador girlfriend for six hours? In the future Lynn and I took her with us, left her in the backseat of the car while we attended functions or did what we needed to do, and visited her in the car at intervals to make sure she was okay and to give her a biscuit. By doing this she heightened my awareness of, and responsiveness to, the needs of people around me, even though I had been pretty good on that score to begin with.

She herself was so responsive to those around her she could read minds. If I was in a foul mood she would rise and go into another room, even though I hadn't said anything out loud and was simply processing in my head a deranged, profane interior monologue. Animals *do* have extrasensory perception. There is no question of that for those of us who've owned great animals. Sorrow, for instance, Dutchie would attack with instant healing countermeasures. I rarely cry since my dad made a military campaign of beating the impulse to do so out of me, but once when I did, when my country neighbor Pete Cameron died, Dutchess reared up on her hind legs as I sat on the couch and licked my face until I was able to stop. But the really great thing she did was help to alter my self-destructive behavior. Lynn for years had protested my fondness for hooch and cigarettes but I had blithely ignored her for the reasons I've cited. Addicts of course invent any and all mental dodges to justify their addictions.

CHAPTER FIFTEEN

Before I tried AA I tried something called Rational Recovery. It was billed as AA without the God business. I'd spotted an article about it in *The Times* and decided to give it a try, reluctantly. After work I jumped the subway downtown and attended a few meetings in Greenwich House in the Village. I also bought a copy of the book this organization put out, called, logically enough, *Rational Recovery*. This was intended as an antidote to, and counterpart of, AA's famous book that bears its name, *Alcoholics Anonymous,* popularly known as "the Big Book." According to the RR people, the Big Book had too much God stuff in it. At a glance it is patently obvious to anyone that AA and its philosophy and its now legendary and often imitated "Twelve Steps" are a rehash, distillation, and condensation of the best principles and teachings of the Judeo-Christian tradition. So by definition AA has much in it about God.

But in AA you can take this God business or leave it. There are AA groups for agnostics and atheists, and people manage to get off the sauce and stay sober using these groups. There is also the AA loophole that "the God of your understanding," as the literature phrases it, can stand simply as an acronym for "Group Of Drunks" or for "Good Orderly Direction." Believe me, no organization has ever loved acronyms more than AA. Their overuse is ludicrous. Hardcore AAs are often characterized as "AA Nazis" and are somewhat like Communist hardliners and just as misguided and silly. The other night one of these AA Nazis asked me how I was. I replied, "Fine." He had no better manners or breeding than to snap his fingers in my face and tell me, wagging his index finger at me the whole time, "No, you are not *fine*. Never *fine*. Don't you know what *fine* means? It means: Fucked up, Insecure, Neurotic, and Emotionally imbalanced. *Never, ever* use that word."

I smiled, thanked him, and moved on. This kind of behavior is why I had such a hard time accepting AA in the first place, but now such sloganeering and bullying to me are so much cant blowing in the wind and so much acting out by the basically powerless. I pay it no mind. Besides, I am *fine*, in *his* sense of the word. That's why I'm writing this little riff in the first place. To help other people who are also *fine* and trying fruitlessly, and sometimes fatally, to cure their painful condition—Fucked up, Insecure, Neurotic, and Emotionally imbalanced—with the anodynes alcohol and "dry goods," as drugs are dubbed in the argot of the AA program.

That's not to say that all the acronyms in AA are useless. I was greatly helped years ago by a young black woman on the Upper West Side who said, "I gotta remember my alcoholism all the time, and what 'ism' stands for: 'I Sabotage Myself'; 'Incredibly Short Memory'; and 'I, Self, Me.'" That has stuck in my head for fifteen years so far, and I hope it sticks there as long as I'm conscious. I like it. I also get a kick out of the acronym treatment accorded to the word *fear*: "Fuck Everything And Run, or Face Everything And Recover." Alternately, there's a third interpretation: "False Evidence Appearing Real." That brings out the "Faith, not fear" mandate. Since a study at a prominent university proved that 85 percent of the things people worry about never come true, I try to remind myself of that scientific discovery every day and leave the mysticism to the mystical.

Years ago I read somewhere that the alcoholism gene is linked somehow to above average verbal ability; this accounted for the high incidence of alcoholism among writers, according to this article, which was also based on research at some university or other. I guess that's right, but I really don't know, though AA meetings in New York

City are chock-full of witty and highly verbal people, many of them capable of coining a clever acronym. But though I like some of these AA acronyms, I never repeat them. I don't talk any slogans, acronyms, or clichés in AA because their overabundance in the program was a deterrent to me getting sober. So bad was this at first that I thought I'd wandered into an Orwellian conspiracy against good, plain English.

AA's two cofounders, Bill Wilson and Doctor Bob, clearly did a good job of coming up with the AA program, yet the program's genius lies not in its philosophy but in its denunciation of anything to do with outside affiliations or issues that interfere with its stated mission to help people get permanently off alcohol and drugs through what amounts to group therapy utilizing Freud's ingenious talking cure, much mocked by cynics but triumphantly effective, I assure you from experience with it. I say "permanently" off alcohol and drugs but, even when the remission is only temporary, as it was for me intermittently for seven years, AA is a big help. I figured out once that during my bullheaded years of going in and out of the program, I was probably only drunk about sixty days or so. That's out of a possible two-and-a-half-thousand-odd. That's why it's somewhat true that the program can work even when you won't work it. It works on you even as you resist or outright reject it.

. . .

When you consider that addiction is built, like a catamaran, on the twin keels of resistance and denial, AA's ability to float your boat even when you won't put up your sails or row is fairly understandable, though totally illogical, irrational, and unprovable. This makes the secret of AA's effectiveness just as unknowable and mysterious as any and every argument for the existence of God. That's why I agree with those heavily grounded yet metaphysical theologians who maintain that the existence of God, if there is one, can only be hinted at by the goodness to one another people are capable of. Pure altruism, that is; and you get plenty of pure altruism in AA. You have to take the effectiveness of this altruism on faith, or face the consequences of continuing to play Rummies' Roulette, knowing that, sooner or later, the loaded chamber will get you.

Incidentally, denial comes in for the acronym treatment too, but with a phonetic fudge on the *k*: "Don't Even kNow I Am Lying." From this propensity on the part of AA you can see how the program and its repetitious cliché-mongering and bromide-huckstering can grate on your ear and your mind and on your ability to listen and absorb. No doubt I was an arrogant wiseass too, and AA itself maintains that defiance is the outstanding characteristic of the alcoholic, so my ability to fall into step, blighted by the martinet horrors of fifties Baltimore Catechism

Catholicism, was severely challenged right from the get-go.

Oddly enough, shortly after I started my on-again, off-again dalliance with AA, Knopf published *The Journals of John Cheever.* I took to this book rabidly, and read with care and enthusiasm the sections on his struggle with the bottle. Instead of serving as a proper warning to me, they spurred me deeper, in a perverse way, into my own besotted tendencies. I would stupidly figure: *If it was good enough for Cheever, it's good enough for me.* I would drink and read the journals and soon augmented them with copies of his letters, two different volumes of which were also published at about this time.

Reading him seemed to sanction my own self-destruction. One thing struck me hard: As soon as Cheever attended his first AA meeting, as a devout Episcopalian he immediately spotted the program's large indebtedness to the best of Judaism and Christianity. The lead speaker at any meeting gives a fifteen- or twenty-minute speech that is called his or her "qualification." Like the good Anglican he was, Cheever dubbed this, to use his word, the "confession." The point is, I deliberately inverted the import of Cheever's booze battle to prolong my own, if only intermittently. The more my novel was rejected, the more frustrated and angry I became with myself, not with others, and the more likely it became that I would convene a kangaroo court for my own indictment, build to a towering rage, and then explode into a drinking spasm, in lieu of carrying out the death-by-hanging kangaroo court sentence I had imposed on myself for failure as a serious novelist. The explosion would at first burn liquid fuel until it fizzled out and I fell back to earth like a spent roman candle, but a soggy one, a souse all bent out of shape by alcohol poisoning, shaky, sweaty, smelly, and unable to hold solid food on my stomach. Toward the end I didn't "go drinking" anymore, as the phrase is used in North Philly, I simply went on "benders," to revive a quaintly archaic word for a drunken tear.

What I found during my seven-year struggle was that alcoholism was a zero sum game. Touch alcohol, you lose. You couldn't outthink it, you couldn't outwit it, you couldn't outphilosophize it, you couldn't solve it with theology, you couldn't humor it into giving you a break. It was a game as fixed as three-card monte as shuffled up to you by the greatest street hustler of all time, King Alcohol. You play, you pay. It reminded me of a dreadful joke played in Fairmount when I was a kid. A smart aleck would say to you, "Think you're strong, right?" In keeping with the macho code of the neighborhood you had to say, "Yeah." The guy would hawk up a gob of phlegm and spit it onto the sidewalk. The phlegm and spit would sit there, marbled

green and white and revolting. "So pick that up, asshole,"
he'd say, and everyone would break out in mocking
laughter.

Alcoholism was just like that. If you were alcoholic, no
matter how strong you thought you were, you couldn't
beat alcohol at its own game. One drink, you sink. That's
what I couldn't get through my head. The bedrock AA
dictum, "It's the first drink that gets you drunk," somehow
defied my ability to comprehend it. When alcohol walloped
me I would return to AA humiliated and defeated. But still,
for seven years, I had that itch to take it on again. Sometimes when I did, for a few days it would work as of old. It
would relax me, it would put me gently to sleep, it would
lift my mood. It would do all the good things it used to
do. Then it would boomerang on me and lay me low. It
would annihilate me. The language of drinking is revela-
tory here. We have a couple of "shots," or "belts," or "hits."
We get "blasted," "bombed," "stoned," or "wasted." Without fail, as with any addiction, you end up "beaten."

An ordinary person, once having suffered a debilitating
and painful hangover, would not readily repeat the process.
An addict does. The reason? His or her everyday psychic
pain is so intense that the addict strikes the Faustian bar-
gain and drinks or drugs for temporary relief. That's why
ordinary people, who don't suffer the unbearable pain to

begin with, don't understand addiction, and why they, again understandably, assign so much moral turpitude to the addict. The "line extension" on addiction, no matter your brand of poison to facilitate self-destruction, is suicide. How can a normal person understand that? The addict, once having been seduced by the cessation of pain, chases that great anesthetized high straight to the grave, though the process of inducing premature death can take years. It's the addict's thinking pattern that is ruinous, and that's where Miss Dutchie, in combination with AA, proved invaluable to me.

The minute I read in Cheever that when he died he wanted to be judged by a panel of Labrador retrievers it destroyed any defenses I had left to justify and rationalize my drinking. My Labrador retriever was passing judgment on me and rejecting me. This prompted me to think, *How lame is that?* And then, when this initial and wrongheaded and rationalizing reaction subsided, I thought, correctly, facing myself and my problem, *How lame am I?*

CHAPTER SIXTEEN

I never count my chickens until I throw out the bones. To assume I've conquered my alcoholism would be to invite it to return. I have been trying to write this small book in my time salvaged from running my literary agency, operating as a book doctor, serving as a writer and as a ghostwriter, and doing any degree of editing, from line to structural. So over the last few months that I've been writing this homage to Miss Dutchie much has happened to put everything in perspective and, sad to say, to incite the old me to drink. I could handle my obsession with the fate of Barbaro without thoughts of drink. I could handle an incomprehensible horror in my home state of Pennsylvania like the killing of the young and innocent Amish girls in their Lancaster County one-room schoolhouse by a sex-crazed lunatic without having thoughts of getting drunk over it. I can scan the list of atrocities bannering the newspaper headlines every day without being tempted to drink over them.

What I maybe can't handle, I'm afraid, is the thought of losing Lynn, who was diagnosed with breast cancer on January 17, 2007. When she called at seven minutes past three in the afternoon to tell me I almost dropped the phone. Of course I looked at my watch and thought, *Is this how I find out I'm going to lose the love of my life?* Lynn was doing the best to hold her composure while weeping quietly into the phone. My stomach clenched and I told myself to stay steady. The result of Lynn's recent biopsy, she explained, was that the doctors had found a small lump on her left breast. That was the bad news. The good news was that if things went well it should require only a routine lumpectomy to cure it. I hate when people use the term *routine* with surgical procedures because it often proves not to be true. In the spring of 2004 a friend of mine, an actor and singer, almost didn't make it through what was described to me as "routine, meatball surgery." Ever since then I wince every time I hear the word *routine* linked with *surgery.*

Lynn is a nervous woman. I am a nervous man. Over the next month we would endure a lot of stress as Lynn interviewed with potential surgeons and I went with her each time. Lynn also did a lot of research on the Net, and we would discuss the results together. But we were both strung as tight as piano wire, and this tautness sometimes caused us to be short and barbed with each other. Lynn's health has been a source of worry for me ever since I met her and she experienced fatigue, shortness of breath, and occasional lapses of consciousness due to having had a collapsed lung at birth and to having inherited thalassemia, commonly called "Mediterranean anemia." Her menstrual cycle was not the normally unpleasant monthly experience it was for most women; it was sometimes far more severe and debilitating. In our thirties when we discussed having children Lynn consulted a doctor who told her the complications for her could be severe, even life-threatening. In the end we decided not to risk them. On top of all this Lynn suffers from monstrous migraines that in turn were exasperated by her menstrual cycle and often left her lying for hours, sometimes for most of a day, in a dark bedroom. Ever since we've been together her fragile health has sometimes induced in me outsized fears.

I've read several times that women fear aging and men fear death. That's laughably simplistic, in the first instance; and, in my case, not true: I fear more loss. I've lost close friends "before their time," as the saying goes. Some died from brain tumors and assorted cancers, others from heart attacks and, to a hideous extent, a great many of them died from AIDS or from the Vietnam debacle. The loss of people who have achieved old age is one thing, but to lose people really young is hard. I learned that early on when my aunt Mary lost two babies, one two years old and the other only months old, and when my uncle Frank lost his twenty-six-year-old son, my cousin Joey, to multiple brain tumors. AIDS devastated friends in the arts and in the entertainment business. Then again, friends of mine from Fairmount and from high school died in Vietnam, either directly or to drug addiction after getting hooked on heroin while serving there, the addiction most likely compliments of the Golden Triangle, Air America, and the CIA distribution honchos, in that order.

Maybe I don't fear my own death enough anymore because I've worked through its paralyzing terrors, though I don't wish to experience them any sooner than I have to. From the time I was old enough to stand up by myself by holding my grandmother's knees she told me solemnly that everyone must die someday. Like many Irish Catholics she was a big proponent of the terrors of death as a deterrent to a life of sin. From her I went straight into grade school at St. Francis Xavier's on the Parkway in Philly and the Irish nuns there echoed everything my grandmother had told me, only they embellished it even more. They told us to hold our hand above a candle's flame or to hold our finger above a match's flame until we felt unendurable pain and then imagine that pain a billionfold and we would have a slight inkling of what the pain of Hell would feel like.

And being roasted by Lucifer was only the second worst feature of going to Hell. The first was that you would pine through all eternity for the lost presence of God. The nuns told us that at the final judgment those on the Hades Express were allowed thirty seconds with God, to experience the Beatific Vision and all the beauty of God and heaven that would be lost to them forever, throughout all of endless eternity. About the time I started drinking as a teen this inculcated thanatophobia really kicked in. It fed off the drinking, the drinking fed off it. Among the great things Miss Dutchie taught me was how to die with dignity. I'm worn out fearing death and have been for some time, something my endocrinologist, a nice Jewish boy, cannot understand.

When asked once what he thought of the afterlife, James Joyce famously replied, "I don't think much of this one." I do. Joyce's cynicism came straight from the bottle. If asked the same question today, my reply would be, "I'm living one." That's exactly what it feels like to escape the deadly sentence of addiction: like living an afterlife, one no longer half experienced because one is semianesthetized far too often from drink or drugs.

Still, I had to alienate Miss Dutchie with my drinking far too many times before this powerful realization finally sank in. That's the trouble with us addicts. It's those two hallmark qualities of defiance and stubbornness working hard within us. Despite them I'm convinced Dutchie accelerated the process of my growing sick of myself. When you grow sick enough of yourself to want to change, you hit what they call in AA a "bottom." I hit mine on February 20, 1998 when "the girls," Dutchie and Lynn, were up in the country and I was embedded in the city on a three-day bender of horrifying intensity. I was on one of those midwinter tears where I would drink, pass out, come to, drink some more, and pass out again. Probably in between I read a page or two of my novel and mocked myself half to death over my inadequacies.

These periods of drinking and of being comatose alternated about every four hours. Drinking had long ceased to be fun. AA in my view sometimes slights the seductive benefits to the alcoholic of drinking when it's in its early stages and cures insomnia, bathes your nerves in a soothing salve, tells you you're more than okay, you're destined for big things, convinces you you're charming, articulate and witty, and generally lies its ass off to you until it's installing a full-blown fantasy worldview in your head whenever you touch it. If you're lucky and survive your cosmic thirst, that is.

If you're unlucky, the fantasy worldview crosses the line and becomes an all-encompassing delusional system. In that case, you can sometimes hear voices, carry on conversations aloud with persons who aren't there, and generally act out in ways unacceptable to society and injurious to yourself. Along the way you may experience delirium tremens and imagine such things as roaches crawling all over you or rats running up and down the walls and across the ceiling. These horrors I was spared. But I hear them described graphically quite often in AA. I also, when I was detoxing, never succumbed to convulsions. I know from the meetings that many others did. Of course, when you reach this level of pathological drinking and you stop suddenly, you go through hell, even if you escape the convulsions and such things as gastroenteritis, where your stomach lining bleeds and you throw up blood.

I got off easy. I never suffered gastroenteritis but my gastrointestinal system must surely have been building toward it. Over the last seven years of my drinking I no longer had hangovers. I had alcohol poisoning. After a bender it took me days to get right. I would be unable to sleep, unable to hold solid food on my stomach, unable to stop feeling abjectly irritable, discontented, agitated, and stressed. Noise would bother me. I couldn't concentrate to read or write. Watching movies or TV programs my mind would wander, whether the program featured sports, news, or a fictional plot. I was crippled with anomie, aphasia, and boredom because I was obsessed with and sick of my self-destructive, senseless behavior. One other thing would occur: I would have what the novelist Michael Thomas called in an article on President Clinton in the *New York Observer* "the hangover hots." Ironically, this condition succeeds the legendary, Shakespearean "brewer's droop." I would suffer surges of satyriasis and priapism. Lynn, loving as ever, would often help me out with this; that is, if she wasn't, understandably, too disgusted with me.

My own disgust with me was a huge problem. That gray and wintry-bleak morning of February 20, 1998 I came to about two hours before daybreak. The first light of that, for me, magical and momentous day would turn out two hours later to be weak and dingy and thereby perfectly suited to my suicidal mood. I was out of booze and didn't know what to do or where to turn. Physically, psychologically, and emotionally I was wrecked, but like a good addict I thought I should go get more hooch. Then I realized that there is a short window under New York law when you can't buy alcoholic beverages. It's absurdly short to someone who grew up under Pennsylvania's blue laws. I think you can't buy booze from four in the morning until six, or something like that, and, on Sundays, until noon. So I was stuck in a cold turkey sweat. I decided after an agonizing half hour, spent mostly stupefied with psychic pain, that I would call a friend in the program who lives in Ireland. It was coming up on ten o'clock in the morning there.

Through some kind of magic he talked me into going to the next available meeting. This was scheduled for six o'clock in what is called The Little Room on Ninety-sixth Street just in from Broadway, only eleven blocks from my apartment. This friend I called has a wonderfully soothing voice and a peerless sensibility behind it. I realized we had spoken on the phone for a long time. I wasn't being melodramatic but I'd matter-of-factly told him I felt like tossing myself under the AA train, the Upper West Side local subway that used to run along Central Part West. Ever the man for gallows humor I thought using the AA train would add a nice touch of literary symbolism to what I considered my now untenable and laughable life. I'd read somewhere that something like 80 percent of suicides are alcohol or drug related.

I figured, cavalier and reckless as ever, Why not play the percentages! Why not join the other Eighty Percenters! But I also kept hearing my wife's voice saying to me, whenever I'd felt overwhelming self-loathing from past benders and mused aloud about the benefits of suicide, "Please don't ever do that to Dutchie and me. How could you even think about it, let alone say such a thing? We'd be so heartbroken." The way I could even think about it was easy for an addict to grasp and incomprehensible to a nonaddict. It's the result of the way a self-hating soul sickness overtakes you when you feel you can't stop drinking like a death-craving maniac. You feel you might as well get death over with. You feel you might as well spare yourself and your loved ones the pedestrian and odious melodrama of watching you slowly and methodically dissolve yourself, awash with alcohol poisoning. Getting rid of yourself all at once strikes you as the gallant thing to do.

For an addict being loaded is like being at war with yourself. I had a great history professor at college named Ray Lorantas who used to say that wars started when national leaders stopped talking to one another. Talking as a cure does work for lots of ailments, mental and emotional. The simple act of talking to my friend in Ireland had halted my internal war with myself. It had clarified my thinking and abated my self-loathing enough to have me get up off my ass—which seemed to weigh about as much as a battleship anchor—and straggle the eleven blocks to The Little Room.

When I got there as usual I sat in the back. The room was filled heavily with working people dressed in their blue or green outfits. I thought of my favorite uncle, my eternally kind and Christian uncle Billy, my mother's brother who had lived with us and who always dressed like that to go to work as an auto mechanic early in the morning. Also present that morning in The Little Room were crack-of-dawn Wall Street types and yuppie professionals in expensive business suits. Sitting there I felt right at home yet totally ashamed. Relieved temporarily of my suicidal impulses I still felt like wringing my own neck in disgust. Sweaty, flatulent, reeking of stale alcohol, atremble in need of a drink, unshaven, belching like a sated hog, feeling so soiled and dirty a thousand showers would never make me clean again, I still thought, *What the hell, I'll give it one more try.* So far I haven't had a drink since.

CHAPTER SEVENTEEN

While I was sleeping soundly in our Manhattan apartment on Monday morning, January 29, 2007, our great country neighbor George Eckstein slipped away in the small hours 125 miles up the Hudson in Coxsackie. He died about half past three, just about the time he and his younger brother Herbie used to wake up and start their day. Herbie had succumbed to cancer six and a half years earlier over the Fourth of July weekend at the turn of the millennium. That was a fitting time for Herbie to die, on America's birthday, because the Eckstein brothers represented for me a vanishing America, a bighearted and innocent America, an America that could derail WWII dictators and tyrants rather than, in the style employed ever since, install them, arm them for Armageddon, then have to wage pyrrhic and benighted wars against them when, deranged with power, they beat their chests like lowland gorillas and defied our imperialistic dictates.

Such depressing realities as losing a friend or watching innocent people die on videotape in unnecessary wars used to induce me to drink. Miss Dutchie and AA taught me there's not a damn thing I can do about such sad aspects of reality, so why get worked up into a rage over them that only drink can quell? In the communications age just reading the newspaper in the morning is enough to induce aphasia. Or watching television news. Or listening to the radio news. Or browsing the Internet for news. Same result: depression, brainlock, aphasia. Right after the current Iraq fiasco opened for business in March 2003 one of the cable news networks showed a clip of an Arab kid who'd lost three limbs to an IED. The reporter, a woman not overly bright but smiling brilliantly, related how, through the miracle of modern medicine, young Ali or Mohammed was slated for surgery Stateside that would fit him with prosthetic devices so good they would permit him to play like a normal child.

While this relentlessly "upbeat" reporter was delivering her voiceover commentary, this beautiful young Arab boy wheeled about his crib on the one biological arm our war of liberation had left him. He was kind of doing surrealistic handstands while whirling his body like a weighty windsock, his whole demeanor a study in unbridled joy. He put me in mind of Yeats's widening gyre and the falcon that could not hear the falconer and the center that would not hold. Then I wondered at what age this mangled boy's rage would kick in. When it inevitably did, I hoped he wouldn't drink or drug over it. Watching him on television twirl what was left of his mutilated self in the air, I wondered too, when his rage hit, if he would then, again like me watching him gyrate, question why he had to be maimed in the first place.

That same morning George Eckstein died, Barbaro was euthanized a few hours later. I figured out from a report that night on ESPN that I was sipping my coffee and reading the newspaper when Barbaro had his life terminated by injection, just as Dutchie had surrendered hers half a year earlier. I pictured him, just like her, having his spirit desert the body as he was rendered an inert mass of protoplasm and bones. The spirit of a great animal is so preternatural that when it is expelled suddenly it leaves an emotional vacuum in lovers of that animal. That night I kept wondering what stunned agony the owners of Barbaro, Roy and Gretchen Jackson, must have been suffering. They had every ounce of empathy I had in me extended to them. I took some small comfort in thinking that they,

like Lynn and me, had probably been insulated from unbearable remorse by the sense of relief one clings to knowing your animal is no longer in pain.

After coffee and the newspaper that morning I hurried
downtown to have my teeth cleaned and a "restoration"
made to one of my incisors. A "restoration" is what they
call a filling at the NYU Dental Clinic. It's yet more language inflation, I suppose, in the age of branding mania
and the aggrandizement of the professions. Going to NYU's
excellent clinic was yet another of my cost-cutting strata-
gems as I flirted ever more heavily with taking up permanent residence on Grub Street chanting aloud, like Allen
Ginsberg's reciting "Howl," all of Chapter 11. As I sat in
that dental chair eager to go home and work on this very
book I was unaware that Barbaro was a goner.

When my appointment ended, though it was bitterly
cold and windy, I found myself wandering home on foot.
I stopped at Borders on Columbus Circle and bought myself a copy of *John O'Hara's Hollywood Stories,* a newly released collection with an introduction by Matthew
Bruccoli, a man I knew slightly and loved to talk to. Because I would have walked four miles by the time I reached
my apartment, I sneaked three Lindor chocolate balls onto
my book bill at Borders as I checked out. I did this despite my diabetes, justifying my self-destructive appetite
for chocolate, as I used to do with alcohol, as a "reward"

for either working or exercising for hours. So the thinking of an addict goes.

Eating the Austrian chocolate was also the usual retreat into comfort food. My wife's breast cancer was eating away at my central nervous system in a voracious way. I kept worrying about her obsessively. I could worry for America in the Olympics. That explains why I titled my battered and bruised and much-rejected novel *Worry Later,* after the immortal Thelonious Monk number. Even jazz, despite its patent divinity as America's ecclesiastical music, could not stop me worrying. And Lynn's illness, on the Richter Scale of Worry, was the equivalent of the 1906 San Francisco earthquake. When I reached my apartment, my hands not yet thawed, I retrieved my voice mail and was hit with a barrage of rejections on a book proposal I had been hired to write. Three of five interested publishers had dropped out. I focused on these rejections and not on the fact that, as it turned out a week or so later, the other two publishers made offers.

I sat down and ate hot soup and a grilled and buttered baguette and turned on the TV. I checked CNBC and, assured by the Dow and the Nasdaq I was not yet bankrupt but perhaps well on the way, I flipped to ESPN and settled in the armchair for a minute to warm up and take a breather. I planned to stroll up Amsterdam Avenue and attend the Night Light AA meeting in a few minutes, but first I needed a brief interval of mindless TV with my feet up. That's when I saw the ESPN streamer with the announcement that Barbaro was no more. I kept waiting for the streamer to recycle to make sure I wasn't misreading it. I think I read it three times, ignoring whatever was said and displayed on the screen above the streamer.

I was shattered but too stunned to do anything but try to stay calm. I had heard the announcement the night before that Barbaro had taken a turn for the worse. With my lugubrious negativity I had told Lynn many times I feared that this champion colt was doomed. Yet, with the deeply embedded magical realism of all Catholics, I had hoped he would survive, no matter the odds against him, and rebound enough to at least reproduce himself in a Kentucky breeding shed by covering mares even if he could no longer fly around the track like the champion he was. I wanted to end this book with Barbaro on a farm, hobbled but chomping grass in a paddock between jaunty visits to the breeding shed, where, in the words of his owner Gretchen Jackson, he would "produce little Barbaros."

Now that was never going to happen. This didn't sit well with me. I threw on my winter topcoat, scarf, knitted hat, and gloves, and started up Amsterdam Avenue, with yet another loss deranging me. I was convinced yet again that God, if there was one, was a sadist. To break my train of thought I resorted to a ruse I had used for four decades. I called Lynn, the sane and loving Lynn. I wanted to tell her Barbaro was gone. Instead she told me she had taken a freelance job I had told her to pass on because I didn't want her encumbered with it at a time when she was, perhaps fatally according to my racing imagination, imperiled with the serious medical problems of breast cancer. I had begged her to put her health front and center and to baby herself. I would come up with any money we needed, I had assured her over the last twelve days since we'd learned of the small tumor in her left breast. I reassured her again now on the cell phone of this financial capability of mine despite the doubts tormenting me from the three rejections I'd just received.

When Lynn told me she had taken the job anyway, despite a deadline only four days off, and that she intended to drive down from the country very, very late that night with heavy desktop computer equipment in order to do the job while in the city for medical tests, I pictured her dropping the computer equipment, falling on the broken plastic and glass, and injuring herself permanently and perhaps—somehow—worsening the breast cancer.

I hit an emotional wall and exploded. I screamed into the cell phone, begging her to reconsider and decline the assignment, convinced now, to top everything off, I'd lose Lynn, through her reckless disregard for her own health, prompted by my economic inadequacy. My mind was racing, my heart pounding. Alcoholics are wired wrong. We go in the wrong emotional and intellectual direction all the time.

CHAPTER EIGHTEEN

Interruptions are the worst thing that can happen to a writer short of incapacitating illness and death. Lynn's illness, as it should, took precedence over everything else. But as luck would have it, right after her diagnosis, I had one book-doctoring assignment come in simultaneously with one editing assignment. Then I had another writing assignment materialize. Plus the taxes had to be done, both business and personal. Of course the job assignments were good news in the financial department, but between helping Lynn and worrying about her I lost volumes of time and had to scramble to catch up on my freelance work. As things turned out I was delighted to scramble for thirty days away from the writing of this memoir because Lynn came through the lumpectomy beautifully. Then she did the new and shortened radiation treatment using the innovative MammoSite technique that utilizes a balloon to pinpoint the radiation. And now she needs only a new drug called Arimidex rather than chemotherapy. As Lynn says with a smile, "I can keep my hair."

So we lucked out after nearly a month of clawing anxiety. My defense had been to go to as many as three and four meetings a day, listening to the problems of others, biding time against the urge to obliterate myself with drink, venting a good bit in meetings, which is unusual for me since I usually only listen. Sitting in the basement room of New York-Presbyterian Weill Cornell Medical Center shortly after dawn on the gray winter morning of February 7, 2007 among the women prepping for mastectomies and lumpectomies was one of the most stressful hours I have ever spent on earth. While the various machines and computers hummed and whirred around me I wondered how God could maim and mutilate these gorgeous women with anything as barbaric as breast cancer. How could something as prepossessingly beautiful and endlessly recreational as a woman's breast be the occasion of cancer? Worse: the cause of her death? The "God of my understanding" is more James Joyce's supremely indifferent deity paring his fingernails than the Bible's beneficent supreme being with his eye on the sparrow.

With the potential cancer catastrophe apparently averted I'm a happy frustrate, if you know what I mean: unbelievably grateful that Lynn is okay and intact yet haunted all

the time by thoughts of failing Miss Dutchie by not fulfill-
ing my need to pay tribute to her on paper. Lynn inadver-
tently fueled my anxiety about failing Dutchie. Throughout
her bout with breast cancer she lamented that she had no
Dutchie to comfort her, to "cuddle with." Whenever Lynn
says this she and I realize yet again that for twelve years
and two months Dutchie was the emotional rudder on our
relationship. Lynn is blessed and cursed with an artistic
temperament to reasonable degrees and, as you can see, I
have issues and illnesses and am arguably crazy. Dutchie
steadied our ship and we had essentially smooth sailing
whenever she guided the trimming of our sails.

Now she's been dead more than nine months and the
sense of her absence grows sharper even as the reconcilia-
tion to her loss sinks in. When I'm in the country with
Lynn and she goes up to bed while I am still upstairs working, I often come downstairs later and find the TV, when I
turn it on, tuned to Animal Planet. A few times Lynn used
my laptop to go online and when I hit a key to jump out of
screensaver mode I discovered that she had been browsing
the ASPCA Web site. We're both badly doglorn. I know
we have to get another dog but I want so badly to write
this memoir of Miss Dutchie first, to celebrate her and ex-
alt in her spirit and wisdom before I get another puppy and
confuse my emotions and thoughts with a whole new canine love affair.

. . .

Three days ago I started for the subway on my way to a business lunch and a woman and her son were walking a ten-week-old black Lab puppy named Mickey on West Eighty-sixth Street. I stopped and fussed with the puppy and regaled the owners with my sad tale of losing Miss Dutchie. I thought in the subway, *Shut up about Miss Dutchie,* but I can't. Next day I went to my Wednesday night meeting of the Oxford Group and a great friend told me tearfully that she had lost her dog. A few weeks earlier while celebrating my ninth anniversary of sobriety I had mentioned the past year's traumas of losing my dog and having my wife diagnosed with breast cancer as amazing potential stumbling blocks I had avoided descending into drunkenness over. Despite the pain, stress, and worry caused by these setbacks I had embraced my consciousness rather than obliterated it.

Lynn often quotes a saying she learned in Al-Anon: "When you are fearful of wolves there's one around every corner." I think about Miss Dutchie all the time and tell myself to complete this memoir and get on with my life— "Get a life," as the twentysomethings snap at one another, unaware their youthful bravado is a kind of ignorance. Deadlocked obsession is life, only intensified. These days I see myself more in Jack Nicholson's Schmidt and Melvin Udall than in his memorable J. J. Gittes and Bad Ass Buddusky. Moving through the remainder of my life I'm more reflective, chagrined, obsessed and cerebral than I am aggressive, arrogant, mouthy, and driven.

When I think of the awful punk values I absorbed in North Philly and how they redounded to my injury, from almost getting me killed to storming out of graduate school, I think of how alcohol always fueled the folly of such reckless escapades. When my mind dwelled on these mistakes and regretted them, I'd think: *Messed up and made a hash of things? Don't worry about it, have a drink, take a load off your mind.* That way I'd tee myself up to make yet more mistakes, all derived from the same source: alcohol. Addictive thinking is as futile and stalemated as a dog chasing its tail. For me such thinking was a shortcut to Alfred E. Newman and his antic but juvenile philosophy, "What, me worry?" In high school the teachers told me alcohol was the universal solvent, but in my life it solved little and, while at it, nearly dissolved everything I valued, including my dreams.

As Lynn battles her way through the aftermath of cancer, whenever she laments not having Dutchie here to comfort her, I remember the major role Dutchie played in shark-walking me back to health. I know how bereft Lynn feels without her. Not only did Dutchie's cold-shoulder treatment alert me to the full repulsiveness of my alcoholism, but her quiet solicitation and emotional reinforcement got me over the hump in kicking nicotine as well.

On March 8, 2000 I was disgusted with myself for my repeated failures to shed the cigarette habit, so I quit cold turkey and haven't had a smoke since. When I took that ill-advised drink in Ireland after five years of abstinence from alcohol and tobacco use, it was on our first visit to "the land of saints and poets." That's the corny way the Irish nuns who taught me in grade school had characterized their native country. Exploring Ireland in 1984 filled me again with my love of literature and I went crazy on the Yeats and Joyce trail. We stood at Yeats's grave under Ben Bulben, visited the isle of Innisfree, bought, in honor of Joyce, lemon soap at Sweeney the Chemist, found Eccles Street and saw a row house across the street from where Number 7 had stood that was the exact same type as Poldy's house, now demolished. This house had the same configuration as Leopold and Molly Bloom's house had on Bloom's pedestrian wanderings on June 16, 1904. It had the same grill-work out front and the same subterranean kitchen entrance like the one Poldy and Dedalus used that late Thursday night of June 16, 1904—actually, by the time the grillwork railing was scaled and entry to the house gained through the kitchen door, it would have been the early morning of Friday, June 17.

That would have made it exactly ninety years to the

day before the early morning when my great friend the novelist and poet Charlie McDade died in bed of a heart attack at age fifty-one, in his Hudson River Valley house in Monroe, New York, downriver from our place in Coxsackie some ninety miles or so. I tell you, the chronometer in my mind is weird. And I use the word *weird* in its Old English sense of being "fateful"; that is, influenced by the gods.

When Charlie died, Dutchie was for me a rock. At about seven o'clock that evening Charlie's widow, Rowena, called to tell Lynn and me that Charlie had been found dead in bed that afternoon when his daughter Maeve came home from school. Like me, Charlie wrote and read late into the night. Usually while doing so he listened to jazz or blues, both great loves of his. It was Dutchess, age four months, who walked with me in circles around our house in Coxsackie as I was trying to absorb the shock. I had been mowing the lawn in glorious summer solstice sunlight, and thinking, as I always did, of how much John Cheever loved and raved about the strength and purity of that Hudson Valley "river light."

It was magical that evening, the light was: silky, bleached, and slanting through the mint green of that early summer foliage. Though the light was uplifting it forfeited its impact on me to the shock I felt. I was brain numb at

Charlie's demise and kept telling Dutchie that things would be all right, repeating it aloud more for my benefit than hers. I was trying to convince myself that I would not miss Charlie half as much as I have every single day since then.

Sensing my pain Dutchie would not leave my side. As we circled the house I was reviewing in my head all the hundreds of great memories I had of Charlie. But it was odd. Toward the end his clinical depression had fostered so much negative energy and fatalistic thinking that I was starting to break away from him in some important ways. One of the most important was over AA. He did not think I was an alcoholic and resented that I had "succumbed" to the "hooey" and "bunkum" of a twelve-step program. He maintained that all such programs taught you to be "self-ish" and turned you away from your real obligations in life, like those to your family and friends. He repeated many times that he had seen me drunk no more than two times in the seventeen years we'd known each other, which happened to be true, and that I was being modish and silly to embrace AA. According to him I was merely following a trend.

"In the fifties nobody would have even considered you a heavy drinker," he told me more than once. When I was on a slip and slopping booze I would agree with him, but as soon as sanity returned I knew he was wrong and defensive, just as he was wrong and defensive when I told him he needed psychotherapy to cope with his clinical depression. His writing was slowing down to a standstill, and still he disagreed and argued with me, resisting and rejecting my altruistic advice. I'm convinced that had he listened to me and addressed his severe depression his blood pressure could have been brought under control and his fatal heart attack avoided. But it was all a moot point that June evening. He was dead.

After nightfall Dutchie and I went inside, and she sat at my feet in the living room as I watched the Rockets beat the Knicks. I watched the game through teary eyes and hardly noticed when the broadcast was interrupted by news breakaways featuring shots of O. J. Simpson's white Bronco leading the LAPD and the CHIP cruisers up and down the L.A. freeways. Though I had predicted that the Rockets would win the NBA championship, I couldn't root for them any longer. Charlie and I were great ones for late-night conversations, two Irishmen nattering away over the phone about life and literature and sports, and I, a Philly guy and a Sixers fan, had bet him the previous night in our midnight yammer that the Rockets would beat his beloved Knicks and win the championship. They did just that that season, of course. So the bet I won was the only legacy of the last conversation Charlie and I ever had. No matter. Even a Pentagon supercomputer couldn't count the thousands of one-sided conversations I've had since then in my head with him, miss him as I do.

CHAPTER NINETEEN

Dutchie was an important connection to another writer friend, one who helped me magnificently when I was fighting the booze battle in the early days of trying to get with the program. That was Gerard Wagner, native of New Orleans, a recovering Catholic if ever I met one. Dutchie loved him. He had a winning manner with animals as well as with people, and he stood six feet five and weighed about 235. A total hippie, he looked like Haight-Ashbury's answer to Dogpatch's Li'l Abner. He had hands the size of Chinese folding fans, and Dutchie couldn't get enough of his rubdowns, vigorous yet gentle and accompanied by a baritone cooing that Johnny Cash would have envied. My friend the painter John Lees once described Gerard as "the kind of man who could knock down a house with a rail-road tie."

Shirtless in summer, Gerard wore bib overalls and

looked at times, especially when he hitched his thumbs behind each strap, like a hardscrabble tenant farmer taking a break behind a tired mule in the rich delta loam of his native Louisiana. Like me he was a refugee from academe, but, unlike me, he had actually stayed in the fabled groves long enough to teach at St. Leo's College in Florida, at the University of South Florida, at the University of Houston, and at the State University of New York at Albany. He was dismissed from SUNY Albany for fraternizing too avidly with the students and for giving anyone an A who needed it to thwart the draft during the debacle in Vietnam. I loved him for that and a million other reasons.

Big Gerard never met a drink or drug he didn't like. When he got the boot from the Ivory Tower he went back to owning and running a bar, Limelight, this time in the Hudson Valley. I say "went back to" because previously he had run a literary watering hole in Florida near St. Leo's called The Wild Boar. There he befriended Kerouac and, through him, came to know just about all the Beats. When Ginsberg and the gang held court at their farm in upstate New York, Gerard left his small spread in Surprise, drove over there, partied and took his cuts in the poetry-reading lineup. Gerard had taught English and speech and coached the debating teams at the colleges that hired him, and to hear him read the English language aloud was maybe a smidgen short of listening to Brando or Burton read it.

His poetry was the usual Beat blend distilled from the Whitman–Williams mash, laced with social protest and spiked with sexual yawping. As a reaction against Catholic repression and his mother's "priest worship" at his and his dad's expense, he flaunted his lust and lured the ladies with a headlong, honey-tongued lunge. He could morph from Li'l Abner to Rhett Butler pretty fast, especially when he donned his white suit with pink piping and his wide-brimmed riverboat gambler's white sombrero with pink trim. He was movie-star handsome and possessed a manner and grin as boyish and well rounded as a baseball. When he got in his antebellum southern planter's rig he felt like Mark Twain, I'm sure, one of his hero writers and also one of mine.

When Gerard died right after midnight on April 16, 2004 he took a large part of my joy in life with him. He was the most effervescent man I'd ever met. Sober he was unbeatable as long as he could keep his rage at bay. That, of course, was an affliction I could relate to one-to-one. All during the years I struggled to write my novel *Worry Later* and to maintain sobriety as a lifestyle commitment, Gerard was a magnificent help. He would roar into the driveway in his white Toyota pickup and off we'd go to meetings, or I would drive over to his farmhouse and eat a quick dinner with him and his indescribably nice wife, Bessie, a gorgeous southern belle, formally named Sarah Bess Stewart Wagner. Her granddad had taught at the University of Southern Mississippi back when it was called Mississippi Southern College, and she'd grown up in Hattiesburg.

After dinner we'd go to the meetings in Greenville, Gerard and I to AA and Bessie to Al-Anon. Like me, Gerard had driven his wife into Al-Anon. When we weren't talking AA, politics, or sports while driving around the Hudson River Valley, Gerard and I would talk about literature. He had been a graduate student in English with a concentration in American Literature and had had a professor at Indiana University, a specialist in Nineteenth-Century American Lit, who had influenced him greatly, Professor Jim Cox. From Cox he got his enthusiasm for Twain and Melville and Thoreau.

Gerard relished any chance to hark back to his glory days as a grad student at IU. Besides what he would tell me about studying with Jim Cox, there was something else he learned there that thrilled me. Another of his favorite IU professors was named Bob Gunderson, a man who used to roar at his students that good writing consisted of "animate nouns propelled by hairy-chested verbs." I've never heard a better description of what good writing should be. Gerard used to roar Gunderson's edict at me all the time, just as Gunderson had roared it at him. I never tired of hearing it, so glorious is it.

. . .

On the interpersonal front Gerard was instinctively, even compulsively helpful and took in other strays in AA besides me. A lot of them went south on him, as I did a number of times, I regret to say, before I straightened out and flew right. When I was coming off a bad bender one time he spent the whole day with me and took me to a concert that night with Bessie and him at the Knickerbocker Arena in Albany to see Henry Paul and his band Blackhawk open for another act whose name I can't remember. Funny thing, years earlier Lynn had met Henry and his band when she was an art director at Atlantic Records. All during the concert that night my hung-over head was pounding enough without the thump of heavy metal, but I was glad to be with Gerard and Bessie and not alone and tempted to douse my brain in booze again. He invited me that night to stay overnight at the farmhouse, but I wanted to go home and sweat out temptation myself and emerge the next day sober, if half comatose from lack of sleep, and that's what I did.

That farmhouse had seen its share of excitement. Big and roomy, it had been converted into an inn, a Catskill Mountains retreat, by its previous owners, and it could accommodate many people, and often did. Gerard fancied himself the East Coast answer to Ken Kesey, especially while he owned and operated, only a few miles away, Limelight. From this Hudson Valley boîte he could sell hooch legally and vend drugs illegally, on the side. Often the farmhouse teemed with people passing through, mostly hippies and writers, artists and musicians, bikers and actors. There was also an annual "burn party," when Gerard collected his own and other people's burnable discards, sometimes including abandoned manuscripts, and lit a huge bonfire, the kind you'd see at a football rally the night before a big game in the South.

Gerard asked me when we first met to help him with a screenplay idea that he said Dan Aykroyd, a friend of his, had expressed interest in seeing. I told him I would, but after the initial verbal pitch he regaled me with, laying out the plot, he would not get down to the actual writing, try mightily though I did to focus him. I knew how much he wanted to be famous and I wanted to help him achieve it if I could. He even told me once that he was "immortal" because *The New York Times* had run his photo in an article about his expulsion from SUNY Albany for fraternizing with the students and defending their right to do drugs. As for the screenplay, alcoholics are the best architects of castles in the air the world has ever seen, or ever will see. I never even got to type "Fade in" to start the screenplay, because Gerard was so scattered and desultory about writing it.

He also had the beginnings of a novel, titled aptly enough *The Burn Party,* but after reading fifty or so pages of it I didn't know quite how to describe its problems to him, which, as a seasoned editor, I can usually do with any piece of writing. But I felt that after I told him it was too scattershot, loose and unfocused, he lost interest in my opinion. Believing fervently as he did that a moving target was harder to hit, he kept his literary fantasies in full celestial orbit at all times as a preventive for having one land and actually have to be addressed.

Gerard and I loved James Joyce, and spoke of him often. Joyce's battle cry of "*non serviam*" had influenced my life to a great extent, and rebellion was deep set in Gerard's bones too, though he'd done a stint in the air force during the Korean Conflict while I had been a conscientious objector working in a hospital during the other undeclared war, the Southeast Asian Police Action in Vietnam. Still, rebellious though I was, Gerard, just like me in that regard and then some, had got me to quit what the authors of AA's Big Book call "the debating society." By this they mean the reflexive argumentativeness that alcoholics can cultivate into a high art of whiplash contrarianism. Like Joyce, also an alcoholic, and like me, Gerard got his debating skills from Catholic clerics and perfected them in his role as a collegiate debating coach. When he came into AA he found fault with everything about its philosophy and literature, the same way I did.

A former seminarian, Gerard had taken religion too

seriously—just like Joyce, and just like me. Then, as Joyce had put it, the injection of Catholicism implanted by the clerics reversed itself. There is no disappointment in life quite as debilitating as losing a fervid childhood devotion to an all-caring and relentlessly beneficent god. For Gerard the final result was an angry surface atheism about organized religions that camouflaged his devout inner belief in what he called "the Great Spirit of the Native Americans." This phrase covered Gerard's AA God "as he understood him." It was the "final result" because in his early days Gerard used to scandalize upstate meetings by roaring, "Fuck God."

By the time I met Gerard he had cooled down and I never heard him roar "Fuck God" in the rooms. But he still loved contrarianism and revolt, whatever form they took, so long as they no longer entailed drinking or drugging. When I stumbled into the upstate rooms of AA angry, disappointed, and confused, Gerard thrilled to my mocking atheism and my observation that no one could "stay in the now," as AA recommended, because time was fluid and the "now" became the "then" before you could even complete saying the one-syllable word *now*.

Silly and sententious of me, granted, just more pure casuistry; but the decommissioned Jesuit in Gerard loved it.

PART THREE

<hr>

The humanist attitude is that the struggle
must continue and that death is the price of life.

—GEORGE ORWELL,
"Lear, Tolstoy and the Fool"

CHAPTER TWENTY

Everything changed after Dutchie had her ACL fixed. She had artificial ligaments inserted in her right hind knee by that fabulous animal surgeon named Paul McNamara. By then she was seven years old, her muzzle was grizzled, and the operation aged her rapidly. Her whole body kind of sagged somehow. Not only could she no longer run like a greyhound but she was hobbled a bit, with a slight favoring of her right hind leg just short of a limp, and when she rose from the floor she no longer sprang from it but sort of cranked herself off it, rising in herky-jerky stages that, when she got a few years older, devolved into little spasms painful to watch. Yet Dutchie adjusted to these facts of life. She coped, as the AA cliché goes, with "life on life's own terms." She became even more self-possessed, contented, even happy, and certainly more affectionate, something I wouldn't have thought possible.

After the ACL operation I feared losing her more than ever. When I brought her home from the animal hospital on Friday, September 7, 2001, the day after the ACL operation, I ended up spending the night awake with her in the downstairs bathroom, where Lynn had built her a little lair of cushions completely out of the way of foot traffic. Dutchie whimpered and cried that night and I rubbed her and whispered to her and told her the pain would pass. I had been told by the vet when to give her more painkillers but she cried and whimpered and fidgeted with pain so badly in the wee hours that I gave her a pill an hour and a half earlier than strictly called for. She managed to nod off sporadically for what probably totaled an hour over the next six hours or so and I nodded off on the cushions as well. In the morning Lynn relieved me and I went up to bed and slept. Next night Dutchess was much better. It thrilled me to take care of her, and when she bounced back by Sunday I was deliriously happy. But she still couldn't walk on her own. I had to carry her out into the yard to do her business.

I had wanted to go down to the city on Sunday night so I would be in town for the memorial service for a writer friend of mine named Robert Jones. He had died a month earlier due to complications from AIDS. He had written two novels, *Force of Gravity* and *Walking on Air,* both well received, and it was horrible that he had been cut down by death in his early forties by this hideous plague. But my plans changed when it was obvious that Lynn would not be able to care for Dutchie by herself. Dutchie was too heavy, and, though the vet had shown me how to sling a towel beneath her stomach slightly forward of her rear legs, to free her injured leg of all weight when she walked, she still weighed too much for Lynn to do this alone. That's how I came to miss Robert's memorial that Monday. Next day, Tuesday, an unspeakably gorgeous day in the Hudson Valley, 135 miles downriver the murderous terrorists slammed two jetliners into the World Trade Center and took nearly three thousand lives.

Missing Dutchie as I do now that she's dead, I wonder how people find the grace and courage and character and dignity to suffer the loss of loved ones to such monstrous violence and somehow go on with their lives. I'm starting to get a glimpse of how they do it. Understanding this grief business takes on added dimensions with age. When I was a toddler I used to barge in on my grandmother in the second-floor front bedroom of our house. She liked to sit in her Morris chair and sew and darn there bathed by autumn or winter sunlight, using a thimble and sometimes a lightbulb as a last resort so she could repair out-at-the-heel socks. More than once I stormed in and found her crying. I asked her why. She told me she missed my grandfather, after whom I'm named. Ed Kelly died at sixty on his way to work at the Philadelphia Electric Company a few days before Christmas in 1948. I was one year and three months old at the time and don't remember it, or him. But my grandmother would say, over and over, "Oh, he died so young."

I would think, *No, he didn't, he was sixty.* I had the same reaction when in college professors would say that Fitzgerald or Kafka or Pollock had died young at forty-four. That seemed old to me at the time. Now in my sixtieth year I think my grandfather did die young, and I think my artistic heroes died in their infancies, practically, and I'm including Joyce at fifty-nine and Hemingway and Faulkner and O'Hara in their early sixties. I'm not just thinking of Bryon, Keats, Shelley, and Thomas Wolfe checking out in their twenties and thirties, or Dylan Thomas drinking himself to death short of forty. I'm thinking sixty *is* young. And as with so much else these days I understand my grandmother's gnawing and recurring and unvanquishable grief every time the thought hits me that I could have lost Lynn to cancer at age sixty or slightly thereafter were it not for medical breakthroughs in breast cancer treatment.

The persistence of grief is simply ferocious. This past spring weekend the skies cleared and the sun shone after a two-week stretch of Indian winter. The days had been leaden, sunless, cold and rainy and sleety without letup. There had even been snow upstate. So when we had temperatures in the midseventies and blue skies Lynn started gardening, raking dead leaves out from under the shrubs and bushes and clearing her flower beds and vegetable garden. At lunch she came in and told me how much she missed Dutchie this first spring without her. Lynn said she sensed Dutchie sitting and standing behind her as she did her yard work, something Dutchie always did, ecstatic as she always got in spring, running around the yard with her half-brother Pete Fenn or her half-sister Caspar Fenn.

Telling me this Lynn filled up and I gave her a long hug. Then at night when I came home from the AA meeting at St. Mary's we watched Sergio Leone's *Once Upon a Time in America* on the DVD. Klutz that I am I spilled coffee on the rug. When I ran and got the Resolve rug cleaner and sprayed the stain, the familiar chemical bouquet rose from it and filled the living room. Instantly I thought of cleaning up after Dutchie when she had her bladder infection a year earlier. But I decided to keep it to myself and not tell Lynn. I didn't want her to get upset again.

A little later when Lynn was upstairs in the bathroom preparing for bed, she turned to me and said, "You know, smelling that rug cleaner reminded me of Dutchie."

"Me too."

The ready way females share thoughts and feelings reminds me all the time of the power of the female psyche.

The feminine principle ignored is life imperiled. Lynn and I had had a mutual Proustian moment, admittedly by way of an industrial household cleaner, very smelly, and not by virtue of an aromatic and enticing madeleine. But still we'd had it, and still it was Lynn who voiced it.

Her sanity inspires me all the time and lets me know, now that I'm sober, that these thoughts and feelings are natural and normal, and don't need to be blotted out with alcohol.

In the fall of 2005 disaster struck when Dutchie visibly started to fail. The nightmare I'd feared for twelve years arrived. It seemed Gerard was no sooner gone than Miss Dutchie slowed down to a geriatric crawl. Then, ominously, her breathing grew labored. It took on that loud rasping rhythm you get from English bulldogs. Only Labs aren't supposed to do that. It first became noticeable earlier that summer when she went to the river and did her Esther Williams imitation. When she climbed out onto the riverbank after fetching the tennis ball she had to drop the ball and gasp for breath. She no longer spun and splashed back into the river before I could even grasp the ball and heave it thirty or forty yards out. That December when her routine breathing got even louder and more unsettling we took her to see our local vet.

CHAPTER TWENTY-ONE

The diagnosis was laryngeal paralysis. I had not noticed that Dutchie's bark had become subdued. Sensitive as ever, Lynn had noticed. Dutchie was never much of a barker. She only really let loose barking when the rabbits and squirrels invaded her yard or whenever she was let out to do her business at night if we forgot to let her back in in the timely manner she demanded, especially if it was too cold or, worse, raining or snowing. She would then let loose a barrage of barking for us to let her back into the house immediately. During horrible weather she practically demanded we stand holding the door for her while she made a quick pit stop in the yard.

Lynn was in the country with her that fall much more than I was, and she soon noticed that Dutchie became reluctant to bark at all. Whenever she did bark, it was faint. The raspy breathing in combination with the faint bark

made her diagnosis fairly clear to our local vet, Dr. Bill
Perkins at the New Baltimore Animal Hospital. She had an
ailment common to aging Labs, a paralyzed voice box. I
thought it was ironic that Dutchie would come down with
a literal paralysis of the voice when I had struggled for years
as a writer to get my voice unstuck. I was stretching things
with this parallel, but I couldn't help thinking this.

We needed a specialist again, just as we had when
Dutchie blew out her ACL. Bill Perkins recommended
the same animal hospital for special surgery we'd used
for the ACL and I told Lynn when she called there to ask
for Dr. Paul McNamara. He had been warm and friendly
and attentive to Dutchie, petting her and soothing her and
talking to her gently and sincerely. She had responded to
him and liked him in her usual demonstrative way. So I
was disconcerted when Lynn relayed to me that Paul had
left this particular clinic and that the staff recommended
a different specialist. Lynn was intrigued that the recommended specialist had a surname that was prominent in
her family tree. It wasn't at all a common last name in upstate New York.

Bill Perkins had explained the basics of the surgical
procedure to fix laryngeal paralysis to Lynn, but we needed
the diagnosis confirmed and more information on the details of the medical procedure to fix it, so Lynn made a date
to see this new specialist. Neither of us then suspected that

this guy would prove to be a total disaster, both as a vet and as a person. In retrospect we should have taken more time and driven the added distance to see Paul McNamara, who had moved on to a clinic farther away, but I had come to believe, mistakenly, that all vets were wonderful people based on the fact that all of them, until we met this cretin, were. It only dawned on me much later that he never petted, touched, or talked to Dutchie. He turned out to be about as sensitive as a urinal puck, and he only acted out inappropriately after he'd sold us on the operation and we had paid the money for it, not before, when he was all salesmanship and smarm.

Our appointment with this specialist was scheduled a short time before Christmas, since that was the first date available when I too could make it. Lynn wanted me there and I wanted to be there. In the meantime Lynn went on the Net and checked out everything she could about laryngeal paralysis. It wasn't encouraging. The comments ran fairly negative. Many owners of Labs had been severely disappointed by their experiences trying to save their dogs from this disorder. Pneumonia was a frequent side effect of the operation; but, worse, the operation had a one-in-four chance of failing afterward if the dog hocked and cleared its throat too vigorously. Doing that would break the stitches used to tie back the impaired vocal cords obstructing the windpipe.

These vocal cords were paralyzed and wouldn't open as they should have when the dog breathed or barked. Left untreated, laryngeal paralysis led to asphyxiation. Your dog suffocated to death. Neither Lynn nor I could stand the thought of Dutchie suffocating to death. To make things worse, the operation was expensive as well as dicey. But Bill Perkins had warned Lynn that warm weather would doom Dutchie. Dogs with laryngeal paralysis could not make it through the thick humid air of a scorching summer in the Northeast. We were, so to speak, on the clock.

For weeks Dutchie's deterioration had been causing Lynn and me tension. I had not wanted Dutchie to have the operation on principle as soon as Lynn told me about the diagnosis of laryngeal paralysis. My skepticism increased when I learned that there was the one-quarter chance of failure. I thought Dutchie was too old to go through the whole ordeal, and that she was deteriorating so rapidly in general that it might accelerate her decline. As it turned out I was right. The operation wound up costing almost three thousand dollars and it caused Dutchie unnecessary pain in her last five months on earth.

What complicated matters for me was Lynn's growing desperation. Though it was clear to me that Dutchie was failing, Lynn was melting down, in denial and in pain. Lynn in pain I cannot stand—ironic this, since my drinking had caused her lots of pain, but why be an alcoholic if you can't have skewed thinking whenever alcohol enters the equation. Lynn's panic at the prospect of losing Dutchie triggered my compassion to the point where I became positive enough in my thinking to believe that this operation would give us another year with our girlfriend. I convinced myself that she would survive the summer smog and haze and breathe freely into the clear Canadian air of an upstate New York autumn.

It never happened that way. Instead Lynn and I had tension over having the operation in the first place, then tension over how immature, hostile, and sarcastic the specialist who performed the operation was, not to mention that he may also have been incompetent, and, finally and most distressingly, over Lynn's suspicion that I wasn't sufficiently cautious in my care of the postoperative Dutchess. This wasn't true. I hovered over Dutchie and doted on her, just as I had after her first operation—just as I had all of her life. In fact, as I had been after Dutchie's ACL operation, so I was after this latest operation, when I picked her up at this very same surgical animal clinic; I was again heartbroken that she was obviously in great pain and just as obviously angry at me, especially and exclusively at me, for subjecting her to it. She never looked to Lynn to protect her the way she looked to me to do it. Dutchie had held against me—and not against Lynn—the pain she suffered from the ACL operation, and she repeated this pattern now with the pain she suffered from the laryngeal paralysis operation. She was distant with me after that knee operation when I picked her up and had to carry her around for a week, and she was distant with me when she came home traumatized and half dead from the latest surgery.

I am certain that Dutchie understood whatever I said to her whenever I spoke to her, and I was sure, throughout her life, that she remembered me picking her up above my head that second night she came home with me and telling her—vouchsafing to her—that I would always take care of her and never let anything bad happen to her. Being the great Pennsylvania Dutchess she was, and nonalcoholic, and having no time for resentments or grudges, she quickly bounced back from her anger at me over long absences, usually on business trips, which she considered a form of unnecessary abandonment, and she even quickly got over her ire at me from the ACL ordeal. But this time, post laryngeal surgery, she didn't bounce back.

CHAPTER TWENTY-TWO

When Lynn and I picked Miss Dutchie up after her laryngeal paralysis operation she looked, to use my mother's morbid Irish locution, like "death warmed over." She had lost weight, and her throat was horribly shaved and stitched like Frankenstein's forehead, just as graphically, just as ghastly. She was unsteady on her feet and her every movement was tentative. Looking at her I was shaken and I could feel Lynn being shaken standing a few feet away from me. I leaned down and talked to the Dutchess softly but she had a blank, hurt and traumatized expression in her eyes. I wondered right there and then if this whole medical rigmarole was worth it, or whether we'd been sold a bill of goods by this obnoxious surgeon specialist. Of course he had covered himself by saying there was the one-in-four chance the operation would fail. Later I wondered if the realistic odds for a dog Dutchie's age weren't more like two to one, or worse. In retrospect I think the creep was selling.

Despite these negative thoughts I told myself to stay positive. I remembered that Dutchie had been shaken by the ACL procedure too, and yet had bounced back. But she was five and a half years older now and she looked so frail I almost burst into tears. Instead I clutched myself hard and held a tight rein on my emotions, the way my parents always insisted I should. Lynn was so shaken by Dutchie's condition she could hardly talk. When we three got outside and into the car, Lynn sat in the backseat holding Dutchie, whispering to her, telling her everything would be all right and how much she loved having her back.

We had to drive slowly and avoid bumps. Dutchie's throat was a delicate matter and the stitches could easily tear out. The drive was about fifty miles and I did it hugging the right lane and under the speed limit. When we got Dutchie home she was listless and hurt and retreated into sleep. We figured this was a good thing and would speed her recovery. She couldn't have dry dog food and she could eat only while standing up. Lynn had to make tiny meatballs out of Mighty Dog canned food and feed them to her sparingly and only while she stood erect.

I wanted to help but Lynn was in exclusive maternal care mode and feared I'd somehow, as a man, screw up feeding Dutchie by making a meatball too big or feeding it to her too fast or by giving her too many of them. I could rarely resist Dutchie's begging and she, like me, so enjoyed eating that I had a tendency to overfeed her. Looking at Dutchie all torn up and listless broke my heart, and when she stood at the cabinet where the dog bones were kept and looked at me imploringly I felt her disappointment like an anvil dropped on my head. I crouched down and tried to explain the situation to her but she looked at me with imperious disdain. It was the look that always got her more bones from me but this time I was strong. She sulked and went to her twin dog beds in the breakfast nook. I worried.

Next day I went down to the city to attend to business, but I turned around and came right back upstate that night. That was on Tuesday, and the next day Lynn had to be in town, but only for a few hours, so she jumped in the car and drove down to the city. I was in charge of Dutchie. I fed her carefully and resisted her entreaties for bones and other treats. I fed her only the tiny, moist meatballs. She seemed okay but when Lynn returned late that Wednesday night she immediately thought Dutchie was too sickly. I attributed it simply to the lingering exhaustion from the operation. But next day, Thursday, Lynn concluded Dutchie was worse. She called the specialist clinic but the surgeon specialist wasn't in. The assistants said to monitor her overnight. It wasn't unusual, they said, for a laryngeal paralysis operation to leave a dog, especially an older dog, exhausted and listless. So Lynn and I decided to give it one more day and see if Dutchie rallied.

In the morning Dutchie was more than listless. From her eyes clearly she was sick. She didn't want food and wouldn't eat it when it was offered. Then she started to shiver slightly. Lynn put a call in to the surgeon specialist but, again, he wasn't available. I had to go out and run a few short and unavoidably necessary errands. When I came home shortly later I went upstairs for a minute after talking to Lynn in the kitchen. She had been trying to reach the surgeon specialist all day, unsuccessfully.

Finally the phone rang and it was one of the assistants from the specialist clinic. I heard Lynn describe Dutchie's symptoms, and then burst out crying on the phone. I started running downstairs to hear Lynn run to the foot of the staircase and blurt, "Dutchie has aspiration pneumonia. They said to rush her to the nearest vet." Lynn was crying hysterically and I threw on my coat and snatched Dutchie up in my arms and carried her out to the car. By then Lynn had her coat on and was climbing into the back of the car to be with Dutchie. I drove us over to the New Baltimore Animal Hospital and they put Dutchie on IVs and started to work on her.

Lynn and I were emotional wrecks. Dr. Bill Perkins, Dutchie's regular vet, wasn't in, but a wonderful young vet

named Dr. Knee was. He told us they would have to stabi-
lize Dutchie and keep her overnight. My insides were turning over. I felt helpless. So did Lynn. I could only imagine
the even greater angst of having a seriously ill child. It
has to be off the charts, since having a sick pet is enough
to unhinge you. Then Lynn wanted to know if someone
would be in the clinic all night to monitor Dutchie. When
told no, she was obviously pained. Dr. Knee, a sweet guy—
from York, Pennsylvania, no less, near where Lynn grew
up—swung into action with reassurances that Dutchie
would be all right staying there overnight, that she would
be checked on and would only be unattended for a matter
of a few hours. This didn't completely satisfy Lynn. From
the expression on her face Dr. Knee could tell she was not
convinced. So he told her that Dutchie could be trans-
ported thirty-five miles by animal ambulance to a specialty
clinic up in Latham, a suburb of Albany, where there would
be a full nocturnal staff to monitor her throughout the
night.

I asked, "How much does it cost?"

He said, "Fifteen hundred a night."

I said, "Dutchie will stay here."

She was priceless to me but there was a limit. I no longer made or had that kind of money, I had had to put the
operation on my credit card, and I had no strong prospects
of money coming in. I don't handle debt well emotionally.

That's why I avoid it whenever I can. As I write this I'm again in overdraft hell on my checking account. Whenever this happens I plummet immediately into a depressive undertow. My self-loathing kicks in and I start calling myself names, like "loser" and "sad sack" and "deadbeat." I also think that I'm letting my parents down on the immigrant dream of college-degree-equals-colossal-net-worth when I underearn, not to mention my fear that such economic underperformance on my part imperils Lynn's chance to have enough free time from work in which to achieve herself as an artist. If she had to take on more freelance work she wouldn't have time for her art. It's a bummer all around, on several scores.

One glance at Lynn's face now told me that she wouldn't mind sending Dutchie to this around-the-clock clinic, but my voice and look told her to forget it. It really was out of the question. Even the possibility of it kicked up in me, yet again and as ever, the image of those beminked rich women walking their coddled poodles and Chihuahuas in Fairmount in front of the 2601 apartment building. I could see them again in my mind's eye waiting under the porte-cochere in winter while the doormen carried their pampered pooches outside on silk pillows to do their duty, less than a mile from North Philly's Third World–wretched ghetto. The elitist decadence of it, as always, repelled me yet again, as it had for half a century. Dutchie was going to have to cope with life and maybe even with death as a middle-class dog, not a rich one. Reluctantly we left her at the local clinic and went to Sharon's restaurant for dinner. We lingered there. Neither of us wanted to go home to a house empty of Dutchie.

That night was horrible.

CHAPTER TWENTY-THREE

I will always remember how reluctant Lynn and I were to leave Miss Dutchie at the New Baltimore Animal Hospital overnight. You feel helpless and irresponsible when you do so. It reminded me of the first night Dutchie ever spent in a vet's clinic away from us. It was during the winter when she was two or three years old. We were all in the city and she came down with some dreadful type of animal flu. She was feverish and shivering and going at both ends. We were cleaning up mess after mess and finally I took her to a magnificent veterinarian we used in the city named Dr. Sweighaft, who had offices on Eighty-sixth Street one block over from us on the edge of Central Park West.

He tested young Dutchie and told me she had contracted a bad virus and needed to be kept overnight for observation. She hated being taken from me in the examination room of his office and going into the back of that clinic. I remember the kind Latino assistant in blue scrubs leading her away, and the forlorn look she cast over her shoulder at me. I went back to our apartment and spent a restless night, envisioning her alone and afraid in a crate in a grim room with dimmed lights playing on the floor all around her.

I think Dr. Sweighaft put her on an IV then too. But I know for sure that he took X-rays because he put them on a light board the next day when I picked her up, and he pointed out to me something I never forgot. A broadside X-ray of her showed that vertebrae in her spine at the forefront of her hips were defective. Squeezed, they jutted above the other vertebrae. Dr. Sweighaft said, "These ruptured vertebrae will eventually be trouble when she gets older." I asked a few follow-up questions though I didn't want the answers. The main answer was this: When these ruptured vertebrae eventually snapped they would leave Dutchie a cripple. She'd have a severed spine. In effect she'd be a paraplegic.

As I indicated before, I'm not a good AA or an effective learner when it comes to AA dogma. I can't stay in the moment. Remember: No sooner had I fallen in love with Miss Dutchie the puppy than I was asking the average life span of a Lab. Already I was projecting her death, her loss, playing the future percentages rather than playing the present game as it came to me. What if I had dropped dead the day after I had made all these actuarial calculations about Dutchie's impending death? Fate or my gene pool or God or AA's Higher Power would have had a last laugh on me.

Here it was early January 2006 and Miss Dutchie was confined to a crate with an IV stuck in her in the back room of the New Baltimore Animal Hospital. The hospital is in a handsome building with blue vinyl siding on Route 9 next to the Coxsackie thruway entrance, about five miles by car from our house but only about two miles as the crow flies. You have to drive in a big horseshoe pattern from our house to get there. I like to think Lynn and I left the building that night with slightly less dramatic body language than Masaccio used to depict Adam and Eve banished from Paradise.

Outside in the parking lot Lynn cried a little and then I asked her if she felt up to going for dinner at Sharon's. She did. Like me, she really didn't want to go back to the empty house. Sharon's is family owned and Sharon's sister Debbie waits on us on Friday nights with lots of jibes thrown in. A local musician, Armand, also plays a portable organ and sings pop songs on Friday nights. The place is typically crowded. We usually have a good time but this night we were all but sleepwalking through dinner, stunned and worried the whole time about Dutchie, three miles up

Route 9 in her crate and on the IV. When we got home Lynn retreated to the phone and nattered away all night with her girlfriends, a fabulous support network she has. Like her most of them are artists.

I went upstairs to my study, tried to read, and ended up brooding. Isolation is second nature to me the way it is for a lot of alcoholics. A woman last time I was up at Delmar for the St. Stephen's meeting said, "Know what the cry for help is from an alcoholic? *'Leave me the fuck alone.'* "

Visibly I was alone but invisibly my demons were perched on my shoulders. Even without a crisis, negative scenarios play in my head with the regularity of rain in the monsoon season. I was terrified for Dutchie and scared for myself. I was already envisioning life without her and pre-living every painful moment of it. I would picture myself risen at midday and standing at the top of the second floor landing hollering down, "Is Miss Dutchie down there? Is Uncle Eddie's girlfriend down there?" Whenever I did this for the past dozen years I would hear the scratching scramble of four paws on the pinewood floors as she scampered from her lair in the breakfast nook and frantically ran to the foot of the stairs for our morning scrimmage around the dining room table.

Thoughts of losing this day-starting ritual, plus a thousand other rituals we had, assailed me that night. Of course I couldn't even concentrate enough to read, so how could

I write? That explains in hindsight all the gaps in my journal for these trying days of Dutchie's final illness, stretching as they did, with varying intensity, from the laryngeal
paralysis of the 2005 holidays to that fateful June day six
months later when we lost her.

Eventually Lynn finished up her phone calls and we sat
and talked in the living room, and then we talked as Lynn
went through her pre-bed routines, brushing her teeth
and combing her hair and donning her nightgown as I sat
on the side of the tub and talked to her, trying to comfort
her and contain my own streaking fears. As I followed Lynn
into the bedroom and tucked her under the covers and lay
down beside her to hold her in my arms for a while, we
talked about how much we loved Dutchie and how en-
riching she had been for our lives and even our relationship, despising as she did raised voices. Then Lynn told me
that she had talked at length on the phone to her painter
friend Henrietta Mantooth, who is part Native American
and part Jewish—a fabulous combination, in my view, of
the spiritual and the wise. Lynn told me that she had told
Henrietta how helpless we felt and how there was nothing
we could do.

Henrietta didn't agree, Lynn told me. "She said we can
talk to her. She said Dutchie can hear us encouraging her.
So we should talk to her tonight. I'm going to try it as I

fall asleep. You go downstairs, honey, and read and relax by the fireplace."

I kissed Lynn and got up and tucked her in tight and went downstairs. I sat by the fireplace and watched ESPN. Then I struggled to read for a short while. Staring into space didn't help when reading didn't work. Skeptical and angry at myself for giving in to this impulse, I started to talk to Miss Dutchie. Then, trained never to lie or cry by my father, I lost it completely.

CHAPTER TWENTY-FOUR

Sleep that night was fitful and I woke next morning hearing Lynn downstairs on the phone talking to the New Baltimore Animal Hospital. I went down and she told me Dutchie had passed a quiet night and was doing much better. Dr. Bucki, one of the co-owners of New Baltimore, spoke to Lynn and said that we could come over and visit with Dutchie at one o'clock. Their offices closed at two on Saturdays so we would have time to see the Dutchess for an hour, but the vets wanted to keep her under observation for one more night to make sure she was sufficiently recovered to come home with us. I dawdled over coffee and read, whiling away the time until we could leave for the vet's. Lynn and I planned to go up to Albany and run errands and shop before having dinner at Bountiful Bread, a restaurant we liked in Stuyvesant Plaza next to the SUNY Albany campus, before capping off the night with a movie.

It's significant how preoccupied with Dutchie I was that I never found time to write in my small pocket diary that January until the twenty-second of the month. Since Dutchie had the laryngeal paralysis operation at the end of the first week of January, that meant I took a two-week hiatus from my journal while I agonized over her poor condition. I try to write in my journal every day after reading that advice while immersed in Cheever's letters and journals. But all the while Dutchie's health was failing I was trying my mightiest to resurrect a book project for a prominent lawyer whose in-house public relations officer had mangled it. I was pushing myself to complete this project and render it professional, accurate, literate, and balanced.

At any rate, I couldn't eke out the time to fill my moleskin diary with details of Dutchie's decline; but maybe, given all the time in the world to do so, I still would have avoided it. The pain of watching Dutchie day by day slide toward death was playing up hell with my low-grade depression, ever on the lookout to flower into its scathing big brother, clinical depression, excruciating, paralyzing, and quite often fatal. Maybe it's just as well. Writing about Dutchie's mortal decline while watching it might have overloaded my circuits.

I counted the minutes that Saturday morning until we could see Dutchie at the vet's, and then when it was time to go I was afraid of what condition she would be in when we got there. As it turned out when we arrived we had to wait in the waiting room with other owners and their cats and dogs. This I always liked. I liked to watch the joyful interaction between people and their pets. But soon they almost all left and the receptionist told us to go into the room at the far side of reception, not an examining room but a small room that led to the big back room filled with all the crates.

Then Dr. Bucki brought Dutchie in. Her walk was mincing and she had an IV bandage on her forepaw where the needle had gone in. She had on her face that forlorn and hurt look I dreaded, the one that said, "You've let me down." Her eyelids were droopy, her eyes too still. She had the most animated eyes I've ever seen on a creature. But now they were still to the point just this side of lifeless. Lynn was mumbling endearments to her but she wasn't responding. She folded herself down on the floor.

I got down on the floor with her and started our special talk, my Dutchie dialogue, our little intimate argot. I told her not to give up and not to be angry. I told her she would be all right. I told her to fight back and we would soon take her home to "Miss Dutchie's house" where we would "roughhouse and see who owned Mr. Monkey Man." She hardly responded with energy, not moving her body at all, but she did start to lick my hands, her grooming ritual with me whenever I got down on the floor with her to rub her down and give her bones when she was going to bed at night. I can remember the cold feel of the tile floor as I knelt beside her in that little room with Lynn and Dr. Bucki looking on, and I can recall the sterile odor of disinfectants fighting a losing battle with the odors of urine and feces embedded over the years in those tiles.

I recall thinking how very cold these odorous tiles were and how very much I wanted to take Miss Dutchie home and plop her down on her warm cotton and terry cloth dog beds in the breakfast nook and comfort her with dog bones as soon as she was able to have them again. I stroked and whispered tenderly to her but she never really gave me that inimitable smile of hers that used to prompt strollers in New York to stop and ask if they could pet her. I told her, "We'll be back tomorrow. You be good and fight this bug for one more day." Dr. Bucki kept grinning and chuckling at me while I exhorted Miss Dutchie to make a comeback, and then we left with the promise that if all went well we would come back and take her home the next day.

Lynn and I left and went up to Albany for one of our shopping, dining, and cinema excursions, but I can't remember any details of the day other than that it was one of those iron gray early winter days with weak light, a cutting wind, and a quick nightfall. When we got home Lynn and I pretended everything was normal but neither of us could stop remarking how empty the house seemed without Dutchie, even though all she did these days was sleep twenty-one or -two of every twenty-four-hour day. I can't even recall what movie we saw that day, and I usually record all movies seen in my journal, and my one- or two-line impression of them. But its pages are blank, as was my mind that night, when I was able, mercifully, after being reassured by our visit with Dutchie, to get some real sleep, unlike the night before.

The ringing phone woke me early next morning and I heard Lynn say, "Oh, yes, we'll be over in an hour to get her. Thanks a lot, Dr. Bucki." I jumped out of bed, tumbled downstairs, put on the coffee, gulped a few cups, and felt the minutes crawl by. Finally the hour was up and it was time to go get the Dutchess.

Overnight it had snowed and the Catskill wind cut right through you. The sky was gray, the light watery and weak. When we got to the New Baltimore Animal Hospital Dr. Bucki was waiting for us. The place was empty. The offices were officially closed. Dr. Bucki was doing the Sunday morning checkup on the animals kept overnight. Having the Sunday duty this weekend she would also check on them later that evening. She is a reserved but sweet lady. As soon as she let us in she said she'd get Dutchie.

In minutes she brought her out. Dutchie was marginally

glad to see us. She still had the gauze wrapping on her forepaw where the IV needle had gone in. Her eyes were still heavy and subdued and she walked like a robot. We took her out the side door and she had to stand a moment in the wind and the little swirls of leftover snow, not drifts, just the equivalent of ocean spume blowing across the asphalt driveway. She was very subdued, very still. Then I led her to the back door of the car, but when I opened it she only stood there. Dutchie was highly aware of her dignity at all times. She hated to be picked up. As a puppy she had terrified Lynn and me once when she leaped right out of my arms and fell four feet to the pine planks of the kitchen floor. We both thought she'd at least broken a leg. But she was so young and resilient she hadn't broken anything, least of all her spirit, which she'd just demonstrated, with her mad leap, was to be viewed by us as independent at all times.

Not so that Sunday morning. She waited beside the car, head down, till I lifted her and placed her on the backseat. Lynn had bought a denim-covered car bed for dogs from L.L. Bean and reinforced it with extra foam padding. It was like a futon, with horizontal cushions on the bench seat and vertical cushions climbing up the back rest and tied behind the seat at the bottom. Dutchie loved it, and would lounge on it forever, sleeping soundly while we drove as many as five or six hours on long trips. Her ability to do this amused my mother no end whenever she was in the car with us. I used to say that Miss Dutchie lounged on her backseat car bed like Cleopatra on her river barge. But as I looked back at her before I pulled out to head home she was just slumped there, like a homeless person shuddering in a doorway, not reclining there with her regal smile like a queen.

CHAPTER TWENTY-FIVE

We got the one-in-four straw, the short one. The operation on Dutchie's throat failed. This became immediately obvious over the course of the week following her two nights in the New Baltimore Animal Hospital with aspiration pneumonia. It started as a slight wheeze but quickly escalated to a full rasp. Soon she was gasping and rasping again with every breath she took. It alarmed Lynn immediately, but I tried to stay positive and convince her it was temporary and that the operation hadn't failed. I simply didn't want to believe it had. Denial again: my good old capacity for denial. But Lynn called and made a follow-up appointment with the obnoxious specialist. When we got there he walked into the examination room, listened to Dutchie breathe, shook his head and said, "Yes, the operation's failed." He didn't have the grace or manners to say he was sorry.

Stunned and crushed by his medical pronouncement I held on to my emotions hard. Dutchie was doomed. We left and drove back toward Albany. I was going to take the express bus from Albany back to the city to attend to business. Because we had a little time to kill Lynn and I decided to duck into Stuyvesant Plaza and have a quick lunch of soup and a sandwich at Bountiful Bread. We ate in solemn silence, saying every once in a while how rotten and unlucky it was that we got the one-in-four dud result. Lynn implied again that while she had gone to the city for a day and a half the week after we brought Dutchie home from the operation I had messed up and fed her wrong and that was why she aspirated her food and got pneumonia and hocked her throat so hard that she broke the stitches and tore the vocal cords in her voice box back out.

I was too depressed to fight my corner and accepted Lynn's contumely as her way of dealing with Dutchie's impending loss. Not only did I have to cancel my impulse to speed-slap the uncaring vet but now I had to accept blame for killing my girlfriend Dutchie from the woman I loved. Detesting all rage and violence means detesting them in me, I know. That was the great lesson Lynn and Dutchie had taught me and AA had reinforced. It was also the great lesson of Christ but it was hard to learn and harder to stick to once learned. Sitting in the restaurant I had to bite back a lot of anger, at the nasty specialist, at

Lynn's tendency to blame, and at fate. I had to suppress every inkling of rage and every impulse to violence. That mid-January day was shot through with winter sunshine and I sat in the bright dining room of Bountiful Bread, among all the blond woodwork and bright chrome on the chairs, and thought of how much AA pushed and promoted the St. Francis Prayer with its unimpeachable line: "It is better to understand than to be understood."

Ever the wiseguy, when I started in AA and first heard this prayer I told Gerard I couldn't have imitated St. Francis, despite having his name as my middle name, my Catholic Confirmation name, for the simple reason that I couldn't tolerate bird shit on my shoulders. Looking at Lynn across the table at lunch that day I realized I had come a long way, even as I realized I had a long way to go. I understood that in her pain she was lashing out at me for not fixing the problem, for not preventing the loss of Miss Dutchie. Some people say playing sports builds character and prepares you for life's problems. Maybe yes, maybe no, I say. But I know it prepares you for marriage. In both activities you go from hero to goat and back again in a matter of seconds.

In silence Lynn drove me to the Albany bus station with Dutchess asleep in the backseat. It's as dreary a place as you'll ever care to be. In honor of Gerard, dead by then nearly two years, I thought of the one scene in *On the Road* I always remember besides the scene of Kerouac and Cassidy driving cross country with the nude girlfriend seated between them in the front seat, to the astonishment of truck drivers perched high in their cabs and looking down on them as they passed by. That other remembered scene showed Kerouac on his way back to New York remarking how dreary he found the old Harrisburg train station. I used to pass through that train station on the way to see Lynn before we were married when my driver's license was suspended for driving under the influence, an early warning sign of my alcoholism that went unheeded by me, foolishly, and a habit, drunk driving, I'm blessed to have survived.

Compared to the Albany bus station, the old Harrisburg train station, even before it was remodeled in the eighties, came off like the Winter Palace in St. Petersburg. That painful afternoon in Albany I got on the New York City express bus at the last minute, just reaching that wretched station in time. The bus was full and I had to sit in the middle on the long bench seat at the very back, next to the john, with its industrial antiseptic aroma, all the way down to the Port Authority Bus Terminal. I was squeezed between other riders, and very uncomfortable, my shoulders pinched forward, but I didn't care. I couldn't read squeezed in like that and wouldn't have been able to anyway. I put my head back and, I hope surreptitiously, and I assure you silently, wiped the tears intermittently running down my cheeks at the thought that Dutchie would soon be no more. In terms of eternity she was in the departure lounge and she was going to take a large piece of my heart with her.

The next five months are pretty much a blur. I remember Lynn had a freelance design job in New Paltz for a few months right in the middle of that spring, and I didn't like her leaving Miss Dutchie alone for hours in the house. So I got Lynn to leave her with me in the city for a few weeks and we had a good but subdued time together, the way we used to on days Lynn was in town when Dutchie was young. Back then Dutchie and I had the ritual of afternoon jaunts to Central Park followed by short naps before Lynn came home and the two of them drove back up to the Hudson River Valley, always a sad leave-taking for me. They would leave me alone in the apartment, surrounded by agency and editing work and writing assignments, until I could rejoin them at the house on the weekend.

Instead of frolicking down to the lobby and pulling me quickly toward Central Park the way she used to, Dutchess now could not climb the four small steps in our lobby leading to the elevator. She couldn't negotiate going down them very well either because the new super, Pedro, kept them waxed to a high sheen. Going up these same four small steps I had to lift her and she, proud as ever, resented this visibly, shying away as I reached for her, and then would sulk at me when we got back upstairs in the apartment.

It got so bad and so sad that she resisted leaving the apartment to do her duty and then would not enter the lobby after she had. She would brace herself on the sidewalk outside the lobby doors and glare at me as I urged her to come in. I used to take her outside at night very late and she would stand on the empty pavement staring at me and not entering our building until I insisted. I knew that negotiating the steps was putting pressure on her spine and in my head I kept replaying the cautionary words of Dr. Sweighaft years ago that her spine would eventually snap and leave her crippled. Every time these words resounded in my memory I wished I could cauterize them away, but I couldn't. Upstairs I would coax Dutchie out of her sulk by bribing her with bones and rubdowns and cooing sessions telling her how crazy I was about her. She would always respond by grooming me, licking my face and hands, until I sensed that she needed to retreat into sleep and regenerate her dwindling supply of energy. Her breathing had grown steadily more rasping, but since the weather was holding steady at fairly cool temperatures and moderate levels of humidity, she was coping. The vets had told us that the muggy days of July and August would be the most dangerous ones for her, perhaps even deadly.

Then in May that spring Lynn made a trip with her cousin Alice up to Kennebunkport to visit their nonagenarian cousin Phyllis, whose parents used to own the Kennebunkport Inn. Lynn had fond memories of visiting there as a child in the late fifties and early sixties, and she had shown me the place early in our marriage when we made a trip to Maine in 1976 when all the news we heard driving up and back on the car radio concerned Legionnaires' disease having broken out in Philly in the Bellevue Stratford hotel, of all places, where I had worked the Assembly Ball as a bartender once, which might have drawn a long-nosed stare from the ghost of one John O'Hara, and where another of my heroes, F. Scott Fitzgerald, maintained that the best pink lady cocktails in the world were made in the downstairs bar off the lobby. Fitzgerald even took a roundtrip taxi from Manhattan one time to prove it to a fellow drunk. They left midtown, drove down to Philly, had a pink lady each at the Bellevue Stratford while the taxi waited outside on south Broad Street, then drove back to midtown. The taxi bill was enormous, but Fitzgerald had proved his alcoholic point to his companion, who agreed that the Bellevue Stratford made the best pink lady cocktails in the world. Free-associating pointlessly like this I know I'm stalling and don't want to write the conclusion of this book.

Two weeks after Lynn returned from her trip to Maine she called me from the country on Monday night, June 5, crying and told me, sobbing the whole time, "Dutchie's not doing well. She can't stand up."

Next day when my friend Alex Hoyt called I told him I feared that my dog had snapped her spine and would have to be euthanized. There was silence on the phone, Alex as sensitive and measured as ever. Then he said, "I've been through it. It's awful. Do it fast."

CHAPTER TWENTY-SIX

The endgame did happen fast. On Sunday night, June 4, I had come down to the city because I had jury duty next day. As it turned out, when I called the preassigned telephone number for jurors on duty that week, the recorded message informed me that I didn't have to report on Monday as planned. I was to call in again that night to learn if I had to report downtown to the courthouse on Foley Square next morning, Tuesday. Free of jury duty that Monday, I worked all day on a collaboration agreement for a writing assignment I had, and on other agency work, then I went to the Oxford meeting at 7:30, which is only two and a half blocks from our apartment. At the meeting I talked to a former student of Lynn's who asked after her and Dutchess. Having no idea at that point what was happening upstate that evening, I reported that both Dutchess and Lynn were doing well. I felt good too on my way home from the meeting. Then at home I no more than sat down and the phone rang. Lynn sobbed and cried into the phone, explaining through her panic and pain that something was really wrong with Dutchess. She couldn't stand up, Lynn kept blurting.

Lynn said that she'd called New Baltimore and had an appointment with Dr. Bill Perkins the next morning. I comforted her as best I could, my heart pounding and my palms sweating the whole time. When I calmed Lynn enough, after talking for almost two hours, to have her promise she'd take a hot bath, watch an old movie, one of her favorite things to do, and then go to bed fairly early, I hung up the phone and stared at the wall. I knew Dutchie's spine had snapped but hadn't told Lynn that. I remembered my friend Tony Scully, a playwright and screenwriter, telling me years before about the pain and panic he'd felt while out walking his beautiful golden retriever, Bogey (whom I'd met on a trip to L.A. at Tony and his wife Joy's house in Studio City), when Bogey flopped on the sidewalk unable to rise. Tony had told me how he cried and struggled to pick Bogey up and carry him home, only to have to carry him to the vet's that evening to have him euthanized. Tony is a good writer and his description of this event had been so vividly told that I'd never forgotten it. Now I was sure our turn at this tragedy had come.

I did what I shouldn't do. After I called the court clerk's

number and learned again from the recorded message that I didn't have to report in the morning for jury duty, I put on my running togs and, because Lynn had talked to me so long on the phone, almost two hours, it was too late to go to the gym, so I hit the pavements. This is not good for my battered legs. The asphalt and the concrete are too hard on my frame anymore. I need to run on padded treadmills. But I was stunned and panicky myself and, of course, what else? I was angry. I can no longer drink my rage into submission so I try to outrun it. I also knew I'd never sleep a wink unless I tired myself out. So I went out running at about eleven o'clock.

I ran on the asphalt tiles down Central Park West, across Central Park South, up Fifth Avenue to Mount Sinai, then back through the park on the reservoir running track from Engineers' Gate on the East Side to Mariner's Gate on the West Side. I ran at a punishing pace that was way too fast for me and for which I would pay the price in pain and gimpiness the next day. It's not just that my football knee would hurt but that my shins would both hurt and my right hamstring and hip would give me shooting pains. The hip, I suspected, was getting arthritic, just like the back of my neck and the base of my spine. Whenever I wrote too long these days, hunched over my keyboard, my neck would snap like a walnut when I rotated it suddenly, and my lower back would ache.

A similar thing would happen in the morning when I got out of bed after running long and hard on concrete and asphalt. My knees would sound like a mariachi band warming up. I would pay the price for this foolish and reckless running but it was better than grabbing a martini and blasting off on a bender because I was ticked off at life. I loved every minute on the reservoir running track, the wind in my face, the silence except for the breeze stirring the leaves on the trees, the lancelike reflections of the lamplights on the black water, the darkness all around me. As I approached the water fountain on the west side a raccoon I'd seen often on my nocturnal walks back from East Side meetings at the Church of the Heavenly Rest and the Brick Church Annex waddled across the running track and ducked into the underbrush after taking a dip in the reservoir.

I talked to the raccoon and told it that "my Dutchie" wasn't doing so hot. I wasn't frightened anymore by this talking aloud to animals. Henrietta Mantooth, by having me talk long-distance to Dutchie five months earlier when she was overnighting in the New Baltimore Animal Hospital with pneumonia, had cured me of my last reservations in this area. My love affair over the past dozen years with Miss Dutchie had made me a regular Dr. Doolittle. When I had my massive psychotic breaks decades ago I had spoken aloud a few times on the streets, even shouted, but that had been involuntary. My talking to animals these days was voluntary and rational, I thought, so it didn't frighten me the way the other incidents had. Besides, since then I'd come to learn what St. Francis of Assisi always knew: Animals understand almost everything you say to them.

Back home from my run I took a long hot soaking bath. Then I tried to read, and failed, and so I watched ESPN all night. Finally a little after daybreak I got in bed and passed out for about three hours. I woke thinking that Lynn would be at the vet's with Dutchess precisely about then. I got a quick coffee and called her on her cell and she answered and started crying. Dr. Perkins wanted to try steroids but he wasn't encouraging and couldn't guarantee any positive results. He would keep Dutchie overnight. I managed to palliate Lynn and she settled down and promised she'd go home and try to work in her studio while the professionals looked after the Dutchess. Lynn told me she was hopeful because Dr. Perkins said it might just be a bad attack of arthritis. I knew Dutchie clearly had crippling arthritis but I also knew Bill Perkins was a sensitive and kind man and I concluded silently that he was trying, with a fib, to keep Lynn from going off the deep end. I told Lynn to be hopeful but realistic.

I really feared the worst. When I got off the phone I felt

even worse than I had the night before. I lingered over coffee, worried and agitated, reading newspapers desultorily until the time came when I could leave for the noon meeting across the park at the Church of the Heavenly Rest. I walked across the park along the running track to the meeting where a woman I admire spoke on a fill-in basis because the scheduled speaker had not shown up. She spoke wonderfully and made me feel better, if not hopeful.

At home after the meeting I pursued my new and only remaining addiction, food. I ate pizza and ice cream hoping to knock myself out. I succeeded and took an afternoon nap, the very ritual I used to love with Dutchie, especially when I was detoxing from nicotine and felt nerved up but dead tired all the time. Lying in the bed I kept thinking how much I was going to miss her. Then I got up in the late afternoon and went back across the park to the meeting I was serving as speaker's chair for. I had asked a young woman from the Oxford meeting to come and speak and she was dynamite. When the speaker finished and we went to a show of hands, I shared too long about my fears for Dutchie and what I'd done by way of running like a lunatic the night before. I said I knew I was going to lose her and I wasn't just projecting phantom fears, a pastime alcoholics love to indulge.

When the first meeting ended I stayed for the second.

I didn't want to risk that at home alone I might talk myself into a cocktail. The speaker for the second meeting, by happenstance, was another young woman from the Oxford meeting. I say by happenstance because I wasn't the speaker's chair for this second meeting and so I hadn't lined up the speaker for it. This woman speaking came as a pleasant surprise to me. The fellowship gives you lots of good friends, believe me. Of course I've gotten all these precise details from my journal. I wrote in it for these two stressful days I've just described. I was trying to focus myself, to write to make myself calmer, to steel myself.

The entry for the next day says simply, "I report on this rainy morning for jury duty, where I am writing this." I was having trouble concentrating on the journal, so I looked up and woolgathered for a while. It was Wednesday, June 7, and, within a short space of time, before I could write more, the court clerk dismissed most of us for the remainder of the week, with instructions to call the preassigned number on the following Sunday night to see if we had to report next day. I called Lynn as soon as I got out of the courthouse and arranged for her to pick me up at the bus station in Kingston later that afternoon. Then I called another friend and told him I was sorry but I wouldn't be able to keep my speaker's commitment that evening at the Twelfth Street Workshop. I told him my dog was in bad shape and I had to hurry upstate.

Through the rain I hurried uptown, packed, and got back down to the Port Authority Bus Terminal and caught the 3:30 bus. At Kingston Lynn picked me up and I remember that we stopped at the florist on Washington Avenue on the way to the thruway entrance, and Lynn bought plants while I got a coffee to sip on the drive home. Dutchie was by now at home, Lynn having managed to transport her from the New Baltimore Animal Hospital by having the attendants there put her in the car in the parking lot and then, at home, by using one of her dog beds as a litter to drag her from our driveway into our kitchen and her breakfast nook lair. But Dutchie was pretty much incapacitated despite her steroid prescription. I still have the blue bottle for this prescription beside me here on my butcher-block writing desk in the country. The label, dated 06/07/06 reads, "Breslin, Ed (4861). For: Dutchess. Give one tablet twice daily. Rimadyl 75 mg." This was intended to cure her arthritis. I loved Bill Perkins for prescribing it and giving Lynn hope till I could get upstate.

That dismal, overcast and rainy Wednesday my sense of unease grew as I drove beside Lynn all the way up the thruway from Kingston to Coxsackie. The rain had stopped, but everything was drippy, wet, slick and gray, the sky dull and the light a sooty charcoal.

Where, I wondered, was the great John Cheever's Hudson Valley light, raked and white, luminous, radiant and uplifting, just when I needed it most?

CHAPTER TWENTY-SEVEN

My diary entry for the next day, Thursday, June 8, is
blank. But I know what happened between the time we
arrived at the house on Wednesday and the time we drove
over to the New Baltimore Animal Hospital on Friday,
late afternoon. Dutchie was waiting in the house for us
Wednesday evening. When I'd spoken to Lynn from the
courthouse late that morning after being dismissed for
the rest of the week from jury duty, she had cried and told
me she was at the vet's and she had been in the back room
to see Dutchie and she wanted to take Dutchie home, to get
her out of there. No matter how hard vets try, those back
rooms always seem cold and zoolike compared to a pet's
snug home. The sight of the other sick dogs and cats, and
Dutchie among them looking so listless and hopeless and
crated, had unhinged Lynn. I told her to take Dutchie
home and she had, despite the fact that Dutchie was too

heavy for Lynn to handle. At the vet's those assistants had helped put Dutchie in the back of our Subaru Forester, and at home Lynn had used her tremendous artistic resourcefulness to pull Dutchie on a dog bed from the driveway up the brick path, onto the deck, and into the kitchen. That's how determined Lynn was to bring her home.

The minute I opened the back door to the house, which leads right into the kitchen, I heard Dutchie's tail thumping the baseboard and I did what I'd always done. I asked the both of us my usual rhetorical question: "Is my girlfriend Miss Dutchie in here, Uncle Eddie?" The thumps of the tail grew louder. That's how she had come over the years to wear the paint away on that spot in the baseboard. I put my computer bag and my briefcase down and went right into the breakfast nook, bracing myself for what I might find. But, lying down, Miss Dutchie looked fine, despite another IV dressing on her foreleg. I started giving her a rigorous rubdown and she started the manic licking and kissing of my face and hands that Lynn always thought was over the top. It tickled me no end and I didn't care who didn't like it, including Lynn. Momentarily I felt all right, but this feeling was short-lived.

When I picked Dutchie up to take her out in the yard to do her duty she was deadweight. I had to struggle to get one arm securely under her belly just forward of her hindquarters, and as I did this her body sort of rolled away from me, listing to the side like a foundering ship. This strained my back but, more than that, it scared me. I knew she had lost all control of her hind legs. They hung straight down, like twin lead weights for a window sash. Realizing this I almost burst into tears. I knew her spine had given out. I knew she was a cripple; more, she was a paraplegic, having lost control of all four extremities. Because she was no longer animated, her weight seemed to have almost doubled, and I felt like an old man trying to carry her. It was a struggle. I was careful not to shift her weight wrong and throw my back out. I told Lynn to hold the storm door, which now had a half screen in it, and I carried Dutchie out into the yard. I knelt on one knee and balanced her forelegs across the other, which was crooked.

Her panting increased and I could tell she was in extreme distress, not so much affronted in her dignity as when I carried her before, but now kind of stressed out over her bewildering physical condition as an invalid. Awkwardly she urinated a little and I thought she was finished, but when I picked her up to carry her back inside she loosed a big stream of urine all over the brick sidewalk and I knew she had no control of her bladder. I suspected this same lack of control would apply to her bowels. I took her back inside and told her everything would be all right and showered her with affection and bones while she lay on her dog beds.

Then, thoroughly depressed, Lynn and I went off to Sharon's restaurant for a subdued dinner. It was one of the saddest meals we ever shared, neither of us saying very much. When we got back home I told Lynn gently how bad off I thought Dutchie was, and that I didn't think she could recover and that we were faced with a hard decision. Lynn had to work next day in New Paltz at the freelance design job, and she hadn't been sleeping well, so I persuaded her to go to bed and get some rest. I puttered about the house, reading halfheartedly, a bit insomniac, distractedly watching ESPN, and then before I went up to get into bed I knelt with Dutchie and petted her and rubbed her down for a while. She woke and started grooming me as usual, licking my hands and forearms the way she'd always done, but this time I felt as though she had just given birth to my arms and was preparing them to get a grip on a harsh reality.

That page in my diary for all of Thursday is blank, but I described some of what happened at the beginning of this book. Lynn was away at work in New Paltz. I was left alone at the house with Dutchie. She was immobile, except when I took her out to the yard to relieve herself. When I did this she experienced only more distress at her shattered physical condition. As did I. The day before when I lifted her in my arms and knew she was deadweight it was emotionally for me the equivalent of a miner seeing the canary drop dead off its perch and knowing he was going to be asphyxiated by deadly gas, or hearing the first loud crack of the main beams and knowing he was going to be buried alive. In my case, instead of fatal effluvia or the weight of the earth it would be clinical depression that would bury me alive. I knew I was going to be in for a hard mental and emotional fight when I lost the Dutchess, and I started to give myself internal pep talks alternating with readings to myself of the Stiff Upper Lip creed and the Macho Riot Act. In other words the voices of my parents came to the fore, a mixed blessing at most times, but in this case a big help.

As I suspected the day before, Dutchie had also lost control of her bowels. We had put the Sure Care underpads on her twin dog beds because she was clearly incontinent. But it still hurt me when I brought her in in the afternoon from a trip to the yard and placed her back on her dog beds only to watch two turds pop out of her. She looked at me with panic in her eyes over this. Dogs are exceedingly aware of their dignity on this point, and I petted her and kissed her and told her it was all right. I quickly cleaned this mess up and took it to the side of our yard and heaved it into the underbrush. As I did so I had a horrible thought: *This will be the last time you ever pick up after her.* It chilled me. Shortly thereafter was when my friend in the medical field came over to give me a lift to the meeting in Greenville, took one look at Dutchie, and said, "Put her out of her misery. Put this animal down." My friend then drove me to the meeting, but I'll always wish I had spent the time instead at home with the Dutchess. All during the meeting I was distracted with what I knew we had to do the next day, which will always be for me Black Friday.

I had called Bill Perkins earlier that Thursday afternoon, before my friend gave her honest but unwelcome diagnosis with the hammer and tongs delivery of all too many medicos. When I didn't reach Dr. Perkins I had asked the receptionist to have him call me back. When he did I told him Dutchess had shown no signs of improvement and that I felt she was in a dire condition. He agreed and I said I thought it was time to put an end to her suffering. He agreed again and told me to bring her in the next day at the close of business, at 5:30. As any pet owner knows, that's the bewitching hour when the vets do their euthanizations, after all the other clients and their pets have left the offices for the day. Lynn and I had talked on the phone on and off during the day, so Lynn knew that our girlfriend wasn't doing well.

Agitated and distracted and obsessed with thoughts of losing Dutchie, I was present for the Greenville meeting that evening in the physical sense only. I sleepwalked and mused my way through it, listening but absorbing nothing, and then waited anxiously at home for Lynn to come from work so we could share our last night together with Miss Dutchie.

Next day Lynn stayed home from work. She called the office in New Paltz early and told them she had a family emergency, which was true. Like me she wanted to be with Dutchie as much as possible. But the truth was that all day long time weighed a ton. It was so heavy it bent us into seeking distractions, and, luckily, Lynn had a valid one. She needed to finish her artist's statement for a show she was in. We worked on it together in the late morning. In the early morning, when I had first got up and had my coffee ritual, I kept going out and stretching out full-length on the floor in the breakfast nook in my pajamas telling Miss Dutchie through blurry eyes all that she'd meant to me. She seemed to understand but was unflappable. She concentrated more on the food I was constantly plying her with. Like me she still, despite all, truly loved to eat. I gave her a healthy portion of my oatmeal and many bones supplemented with slices of a roast chicken we'd bought at the supermarket. She was loving it. I was tortured.

The night before I was tortured too. I hadn't wanted to go to sleep, knowing I would never hear her breathing in the kitchen, sighing in her sleep, as I came out to replenish my decaffeinated coffee as I read late in the living room.

Finally I had gone in and sat on the john in the downstairs bathroom, which is on the opposite side of the kitchen from the breakfast nook, and, holding my head in my hands, I had whispered to her how much I'd miss her but that I couldn't stay awake any longer. I was just exhausted, all in. It was age. When I was younger I would easily have stayed up all night, as upset as I was. So I had gone up to bed and managed to sleep for about four hours. But, up early a few hours later on Friday morning, I was heart-racingly aware of what this dreadful day had in store for us.

The morning was overcast and slightly rainy. Then the early afternoon was cloudy and dreary. I finally decided, when Lynn thanked me for my help with her artist statement and said she would simply polish it a bit more, that the thing to do was to clean up and take the trash and the recyclables to the transfer station on the far side of town. This whole process takes an hour or an hour and a half round trip, from gathering the trash to bundling it, to driving it over, dumping it, and driving home. I got back about 3:30 and while I was at the transfer station the sun burst through the cloud cover and the sky cleared to a washed and brilliant June blue. As soon as I pulled into our driveway I called to Lynn and she came down to the kitchen. I told her we were taking Miss Dutchie out to sit by her favorite lilac bush, the one I always "hid" behind when we played hide-and-seek.

Lynn thought that was an inspired idea, and she got one of Dutchie's beds out of the breakfast nook and took it across the yard to the lilac bush in front of her studio. I picked Miss Dutchie up and followed her out. Then we all sat there together for hours. I had bought another roast chicken at the supermarket on my way home from the transfer station and Lynn brought it out with a carving knife and Dutchie and I went to work on it. When we polished it off Dutchie hunkered down for a nap. I stared at the sky, watching as early summer clouds wafted by, changing shapes. A light, single-engine plane came by and buzzed through the clouds above us. I might have dozed off but I doubt it. I was hyper and kept thinking that these were my last moments with Miss Dutchie. Every once in a while, stretched out on the ground beside her, I stole glances at my watch and calculated the time we had left together.

At one point Dutchie's half-brother Pete Fenn and her half-sister Caspar Fenn came over into the yard, but animals have a sixth sense, and they did not approach Dutchie, as they always did before her spine collapsed. She sensed their presence and awakened but, though they used to sniff each other out and exchange licks every time they met, Pete and Caspar stayed about thirty feet away and then went back to their yard behind ours. They didn't even bother to work me for treats, the way they always did. They knew something was wrong. Dogs are nothing if not sensitive, and Labs especially so. Charlie McDade used to say that animals avoided sick animals and sensed death. I guess he was right.

I was left alone with Dutchie until Lynn came out of the house and asked me if I wanted her to take a picture of us together. I told her no, this wasn't how I wanted to remember Dutchie. But I would come to regret that decision. Lynn was always right in situations like this but I never learn, so I nixed it as a bad idea. Instead I jumped up and scrambled into the house and up to my study, where I searched frantically for a beautiful copy I had recently bought of the Oxford University Press edition of *The Book of Common Prayer*. I had bought it remaindered for only five bucks at The Book House in Stuyvesant Plaza in Albany. But I couldn't find it though I saw later that night that it was sitting in plain sight right on my desk. Panicky and realizing that my time with Dutchie was running out, I ran back downstairs and out into the yard to be with her.

Lynn went back in the house again. I think she didn't want to lose her composure in public, so she went inside to quietly weep a little and not upset Dutchie and me. I don't know. I never asked her. I'm just guessing. As 5:30 approached, about a half hour before, Lynn came out and sat down on Dutchie's other side and petted and stroked her. I kept staring at the sky, thinking how beautiful the sky was, and the clouds, and what a downer it must be to

leave this earthy realm. At a few points during the afternoon, while I lay there occasionally talking aloud but
softly to Dutchie, I had to swish a silent tear off either
cheek, but when, with my eyes closed, I heard Lynn say
softly, "We better go, honey," I knew instantly she was
right.

I got up and picked Dutchie up in my arms and gave
her a kiss on the head and walked her the few steps to the
car and put her in the backseat. Lynn got in beside her and
I got behind the wheel. I drove slowly through town, with
the vaunted bright Hudson River Valley light pouring
down on us in all its early summer glory. I drove to the
sound of the words in my own head. They were the words
of Reinhold Niebuhr's great prayer, the Serenity Prayer,
the one most New York City AA meetings end with. As
a casual pantheist I wouldn't track as a character in fiction.
I have, all told, about half a dozen copies each of the King
James Bible and of *The Book of Common Prayer,* not to mention my red leather-bound copy from the Oxford University Press of the official *Anglican Hymn Book,* a gift from a
great British friend. Christianity in its pure and true form
is so beautiful it's breathtaking.

Have no doubt of this: I had a tight hold on my insides.
When we got to the New Baltimore Animal Hospital I sent
Lynn in to ask if it was all right to bring Miss Dutchie in

now. I didn't want to spook any other pet owners, or their pets. What Dutchie was there for was clear from one quick look. Lynn came out and said they said to bring her in. I picked her up and walked in. We waited on the blue plastic bench in the reception area, the same room I used to sit in and wonder if I would have such a day as this in this very room, right from the beginning, when I first brought Dutchie there as a puppy twelve years ago to register her as a patient. We waited a few minutes and then they told us to take her into the first examining room, the one right next to the floor scale where they used to weigh her.

We went in and Lynn spread Dutchie's favorite dog blanket, a red fluffy one, under her on the examination table. Then Bill Perkins came in and examined her quickly and said she appeared to be in severe distress. He noted this despite Dutchie's tail beating a happy rhythm off the Formica top of the examining table. She was glad to see him as she had been glad to see the veterinary assistant, a young woman who had met us in the examining room before he entered. He explained what I knew: that Dutchie wasn't going to recover and that her discomfort would only grow worse. With euphemisms all around we consented that she had to be euthanized. Then Bill asked if we wanted to be present. Lynn and I said yes. He explained that it could be traumatic if you weren't used to it. "It will be quick," he said. "But her head will jerk and you may find it unpleasant to watch. She will be falling asleep and not understanding why. Okay?"

We agreed and were told we had to sign forms. I was holding Dutchie and stroking her and talking to her softly. Bill went back out and returned in what was probably two or three minutes but felt like a month and a half. Like a trouper Lynn took the forms, read them, and signed them. Bill went out again and returned just as quickly as before but it felt even longer, agonizingly long. I was breathing deeply through my nose and looking for the needle the minute he walked back in the room. He hesitated a second and I nearly shouted, "Do this with all due dispatch, god-damnit."

Instead I clenched my teeth and stared at the needle. Then he inserted it and in seconds Dutchie's tail stopped thumping and Lynn, crying, said, "Goodbye, Dutchie, we love you." I'll hear those words on my own deathbed. Then I repeated them exactly as Lynn had said them. Then I repeated them again as Dutchie's head bobbed and then sank forward. Bill Perkins put a stethoscope to her chest and I couldn't say the words *Is she gone?* I was shaking too hard and I fought for control and suddenly the room whirled and I feared I'd faint. He nodded at us and that was it. He said he was sorry and she was a great dog.

That's a total understatement but I appreciated his kindness. He and the young woman assistant asked us if we wanted a moment alone with Dutchie and we said that we did. It was twelve minutes to six.

We had both held her after the insertion of the needle and we continued to touch her, our hands resting on her back. She had gone over on her left side and just lay there inert. Then Bill and the assistant left and we didn't say anything but just cried a little. I stared at Dutchie's still head canted on its side on the table with a pink crescent of her dead tongue protruding from her mouth. It was the same tongue, once so animated, that used to lick me with such unchecked affection. After a while the assistant returned with a small pair of scissors and asked if we wanted a lock of her hair. Lynn said yes.

I offered to carry Dutchie into the back but before the assistant could answer, Bill came back into the room and, overhearing me, said he would take care of it. I had always planned to bury Miss Dutchie in the backyard but suddenly over the last two days I knew I couldn't do it. So we had signed papers a few minutes earlier to have her cremated and I now asked a few anxious questions about that. I had this sudden flashback to how disrespectful to the dead the orderlies used to be at the hospital where I worked my alternate service and I didn't want Miss Dutchie disrespected in death.

When my questions were answered I suddenly turned heel and went out to the receptionist and took out my wallet to pay the bill. She whispered to me that the bill would be sent. I sat down on the long blue plastic bench against the far wall of the reception room and stared into the open door of examination room number one, where Dutchie clearly lay visible and lifeless, her back to me. Lynn was still in the room, talking to the young woman. I sat on that hard plastic bench and wondered where Miss Dutchie's spirit and soul had gone. One minute she'd been inspirited with life, the next stone dead. All of that divine touch of life must have gone somewhere.

I kept hearing over and over in my head that phrase: *Be still and know that I am God.* I hoped I wasn't going delusional or psychotic. I hoped I wouldn't have another break with reality. Oddly, fearing a crack-up, I had never felt so calm.

CHAPTER TWENTY-EIGHT

When we left the vet's Lynn and I felt relief. We talked sparingly on the short ride home but that was the gist of what we felt. As we climbed out of the car Lynn suggested that we walk down the road to the cemetery and back. This was one of Dutchie's favorite rituals. All the time we walked we recalled all the habits she had on this familiar walk, the quartering of the fields to either side of the road, the ditches she used to love to frolic in, especially when they were full of dirty rainwater, the rabbits and even the occasional deer she used to light out after. In my head I felt that surreal stillness I had felt after hard hits when playing football or after taking a really nasty punch in a street fight. After the initial ringing in your head there always followed a hyperaware stillness. The earth seemed still, every sound magnified, colors especially bright; even small movements, like leaves on the trees swayed by a breeze, seemed more distinct, more noticeable.

On that lonely walk our mood was reminiscential, our attitude grateful. Neither of us could say enough about how much joy and fun and cohesion and increased love and affection Dutchie had brought into our lives. This magnificent little dog had brought me out of myself and into life, all by herself, with just her voracious grasp of how much life itself could be worth living fully, when fully aware, and not while chemically altered and riven with depression.

Walking with Lynn I knew I wasn't going to wig. I told her I wanted to go to the candlelight AA meeting that night up in Albany. It was already too late for me to make the Selkirk AA meeting in the Dutch Reform Church on 9W, where I had so many good friends who'd helped me a lot over the years, especially with Dutchie's final illness. Lynn said she wanted to come with me. I thought that was a great idea. We had time to grab a quick dinner at Sharon's and to drive to the "Thank God I'm Free" AA meeting on Western Avenue at the New Covenant Presbyterian Church. In a way we were reluctant to go indoors. It was one of those glorious early summer evenings when everything seems scrubbed and new and awash with radiant light. June is like that, the green still emerald and bright, though not quite Frost's immortally apt "nature's first green is gold," one of my favorite lines of poetry.

We duly went to Sharon's. Then we drove up to Albany and I had to look at the New Baltimore Animal Hospital on the way and picture Dutchie in there on a cold slab in a freezer. Still I was composed, though stunned. And I remained stunned and composed all through the meeting with the candlelight playing on the walls and windows of the big parish room at the church. Lynn and I sat side by side and I shared a bit with the group about how tough it was to lose our dog. Then we left and drove down the thruway. While we were up on the northern side of Albany some thirty miles away a violent thunderstorm had whipped and lashed its way through Coxsackie. The night sky was bruised and torn with patches of reflected moonlight shooting down from the clouds. There were huge puddles everywhere and broken tree branches strewn everywhere, even on the highway. I thought ironically of reading Jim Bishop's corny and evanescent "classic" back in high school, *The Day Christ Died,* and how sappy and schmaltzy his description had been of the weather following the crucifixion. Still, I found myself saying to Lynn as I drove into our driveway, "Even Mother Nature knows Miss Dutchie died tonight."

Next morning the weather was like early autumn. The air was Canadian light and cool, like late September or early October. The light was spectacular. Yet, in early June, bright and green and blooms aglow all around, it was chilly enough that you needed a long-sleeved shirt. In agony I sat in my chair beside the fireplace, sipping coffee and feeling jumpy, staring at the treetops beyond the four bay windows. My nerves were jangled and I rushed up to the point of tears a thousand times only to pull back and mutter angrily. This was the same pattern I'd followed the day after Charlie McDade died and the day after Gerard Wagner died, my two great writer buddies. I hated being sober and feeling this much pain. But I knew I couldn't drink and was grateful I couldn't. Besides, I couldn't let two great "sponsors" like Gerard and Miss Dutchie down.

Lynn had gone earlier that morning to work on the freelance design assignment in New Paltz, even though it was Saturday. So I was alone in the quiet and empty house. When Lynn had awakened at eight that morning I had been lying awake beside her giving her the big fish eye as she slept, thinking how much I loved her. During the night I think I nodded off two or three times but I would bolt awake seeing Dutchie fighting back against the fatal injection, her head bobbing, shaking and drooping against her will, as the barbiturates bit into her final consciousness and then took her away. I kept flashing on her grinning even wider and thrashing her tail even harder the second time Bill Perkins entered the room with the big hypodermic clutched in his hand. She was just so happy to see him, despite her spine being snapped, despite being a paraplegic, despite being engaged in taking her last rasping breaths on earth, thanks to laryngeal paralysis. Right to the end she was magnificent, still sucking the joy out of every living moment, still savoring the now, still availing herself of an opportunity to interact with love and affection with another living being, in this case a lethal vet. Until her final moments she was still setting an example for me, still teaching me how to live, and this time how to die.

I got out of the chair when my misery became too great and decided to run my anger into the ground. I pulled on my jogging gear and went for a hard jog. I didn't think about where I was running and before I knew it I had run the length of Riverside Drive all the way into town and around Riverside Park. That's where I lost it and started to cry, visualizing Miss Dutchie fetching tennis balls and sticks in the park next to the bandstand and running into the river down the boat launch incline. Lynn is convinced that Dutchie blew out her ACL spinning after a Frisbee with a group of young kids in Riverside Park. Playing with those kids, Dutchie used to be able to stop and change direction on a dime, just like Barry Sanders, the Hall of Fame Lions halfback. Shifty she could do, and leaping and grasping the Frisbee in her mouth facing in one direction and hitting the ground and running in the opposite direction she could also do almost faster than the eye could follow, like a trick of lapsed-time photography.

Watching a young Miss Dutchie do this with squealing boys and girls pursuing her without a chance of catching her was as aesthetically pleasing to me as watching a gorgeous Thoroughbred turn on at the top of the stretch. It would fill me with a giddy awe and wonder, and I never saw a creature—animal or human—have so much fun as Miss Dutchie had when playing like this with young children. Seeing it all in my head again I cried quietly as I ran home as hard as I could, trying futilely to transfer my pain from my head, heart, and soul to my legs and my side, but I didn't succeed.

This trick of running too fast, to try to kill my anger, was what had really cost me seven months later. When I ran thunderously fast when Lynn was diagnosed with breast cancer I seriously damaged my right leg. I had to make a doctor's appointment with an orthopedic specialist to see if he could find out what had gone wrong with this injured leg. I couldn't run on it and being idle was killing me. I'm also too heavy because of this lack of exercise and it's deadly for my diabetes being fat and inactive. In turn my anger at being fat and inactive is triggering me to overeat, so I had managed with a single reckless and impulsive action to compound all my problems. Being an addict is an all around pain in the ass, let me assure you. Throw

Type 2 diabetes into the mix and you're back with your self-destructive impulses at the wheel and none other than yourself along for the ride in the death seat. I've found that you can't run fast enough, far enough, or long enough to escape yourself.

At home I cooled down and did some sit-ups and lifted my barbells in the basement, then I went upstairs and soaked in a hot tub. I started to cry and decided to shave, not a smart move. I managed to cut myself badly, my hand was shaking so hard with rage, and blood turned the bath-water pink and splashed in bright red spots along the rim of the tub. I had a hard time stopping the bleeding and wondered how I could be so stupid as to shave while crying and shaking. This made me extra furious at myself, the way a broken shoelace could send me on a bender. With me it's the little frustrations that ignite the big implosions. I managed to use a styptic stick so lavishly that I finally stanched the bleeding, cleaned up the tub, got dressed and went back downstairs to stare and brood in my favorite chair. Then the phone rang and it was Chris Warren, as kind a human being as ever drew breath. She asked after Dutchie. I managed to tell her what had happened. She was not surprised and said that everyone noticed that Dutchie was failing even if Lynn and I were having a hard time acknowledging it. She said she was sure we had done the best thing for Dutchie. I said, "It was awful," and then, my mooring slipping emotionally, I quickly got off the phone.

I whiled away the afternoon, trying to nap but not succeeding, hoping sleep would dull the pain but achieving only closed eyes with scenes of Dutchie dying playing in stereo on both undersides of my eyelids. Lynn called to say she'd be home in time for me to take the car to meet an AA friend for dinner before we both went to the seven-thirty meeting at St. Mary's in Coxsackie. I keep things this friend says to me all the time at the forefront of my mind. The biggest one is this: "There is only one mistake you can make, Ed. Always remember that. It's to take a drink." When I went upstairs to freshen up to meet him about the time I knew Lynn would pull into the drive, I checked my face in the bathroom mirror. It wasn't too puffy or red-eyed from crying, but my chin was caked with white styptic chalk dried to a crust. I looked like an actor, clown, or mime in partial makeup.

That was all right with me. I especially loved actors for their unbreakable courage and nerve. They demonstrated this collectively with their right headed and right hearted liberal stands politically, and personally I owed them a big debt because so many of them spoke out all the time boldly and altruistically about their addictions. They passionately broke their anonymity and violated their own privacy with astonishing regularity and valor in the cause of helping others. These twin passions of theirs had brought down a lot of contumely on their heads, and even scorn and contempt, but still they pressed on, undaunted, despite being carrion feasts for the rapacious paparazzi. I've always found actors to be the ballsiest guys and girls around. And the most creative sometimes too. Witness my two favorite movie soliloquies, both written by actors: unaccredited Orson Welles on the cuckoo clock in *The Third Man* and Matt Damon in his geopolitical précis with the CIA recruiter in *Good Will Hunting*.

Shortly after Miss Dutchie died Lynn's mom fell sick and was hospitalized. We drove quickly to Middleburg, Pennsylvania to help her. I stayed an extra week since she needed someone to be with her after she was released from the hospital, and Lynn had to return to her freelance job in upstate New York. While in Middleburg I went to many meetings. When I was new in AA and merely auditing the program, and failing to get it, I never went to meetings in Middleburg or Philadelphia for fear of embarrassing family members with my failure to deal with life plain and raw and unbuffered by booze. But after a while I no longer cared. Gerard had told me this would happen because it had happened to him and in many ways we were so much alike. Just like those actors and actresses who invade their own privacy to help others I don't prize anonymity about being an alcoholic. I'm discreet about it but I don't make a federal case of its secrecy. If acknowledging it here publicly helps even one other person it's worth it to me. This kind of openness, as those actors and actresses know, is a kind of theology in action, a form of divinely inspired altruism. It's not, as those celebrities are often accused of being, indulgent, narcissistic, and exhibitionist.

One such act of openness took a long time to germinate for me, but for it I will always be grateful. In the eighties, when I was dry for five years on my own recognizance, I read and reread Elmore Leonard's interview in a book on alcoholism called *The Courage to Change*. We published it in paperback when I was working at Warner Books. We also published Elmore Leonard's own books back then. That's how I was lucky enough to meet him. Not only is he a fantastic writer but a fantastic man. He was fun to talk writing with, especially about research, but he was even more helpful to me with that published interview on his alcoholism. Since then I've thanked him for his honesty and forthrightness in doing that interview because it really stuck with me, haunted me in fact, influenced my thinking, and maybe even saved my ass from terminal dipsomania. It's possible. Acts of courage resonate.

All during my stay in Middleburg right after Dutchie died I was still shell-shocked from her loss, but I kept a lot of feelings to myself as I drove to meetings. Central Penn-sylvania is inspiringly beautiful: rich farm country with rolling fields and round-shouldered mountains and deep valleys that offer head-snapping vistas. One night I went to a meeting at the United Church of Christ in Mifflinburg, the next town over from Middleburg. In AA in Snyder County they ask newcomers if they'd like a list of mem-bers' phone numbers. I said I would. The moderator said, "Well, all the guys'll give you their numbers." I said, "I'd like the women's numbers too." This caused the whole meeting to fall out in knee-slapping laughter. Finally the moderator said, very knowing, very worldly, "Nice try, buddy. But that trick ain't gonna work around here."

Country people see too much animal husbandry in those barnyards. In New York City and in upstate New York I have dozens and dozens of women's phone numbers who are in AA. I guess this is why Shakespeare used the euphemism "country matters" sometimes when referring to things sexual. At any rate this church in Mifflinburg had a banner hanging on the wall out front that contained a single quote from my favorite comedienne of all time, Gracie Allen. I had never read it before: "Never place a period where God has placed a comma."

I took this to heart. Friends wishing to be helpful had told Lynn and me to "get another dog right away." We will eventually. We're too doglorn not to. But we couldn't do it right away. We needed time. I needed time especially to think about Miss Dutchie, to contemplate all she'd done for me, to absorb all her lessons and internalize them, to "own them" to use the silly cliché people throw around all the time now. Before another dog came into my life I had to celebrate Miss Dutchie. I thought how nothing ever interfered permanently with Dutchie's quest to live life fully as it unfolded no matter what came her way. She couldn't have cared a tinker's damn that that breeder had told me her front legs were ever so slightly too short to ever have qualified her as a show dog. She never dwelled on shortcomings or mistakes, the way I would obsess about the many I'd made in my life, always related somehow to alcohol; nor would she, like me for many years, follow my unwavering and illogical reaction to this senseless remorse and promptly drink over it. Ironic, that is.

It's also ironic that in my life I've been a conscientious objector and yet in my publishing career I worked end-lessly and always happily with so many military writers, usually retired servicemen. They're as good as it gets. You can't meet better people. Unpretentious, honest and di-rect, unshowily sensitive and always helpful, they never let you down, most of them generous to a fault, yet nearly always, in my view, willing to be sacrificed or misused by cynical and corrupt and uncaring and greedy politicians and warmongers, who often throw away the lives of these brave men and women like so much used ammunition, like empty shell casings.

I'll never get that, the unquestioning loyalty these service people bring to benighted and unnecessary wars of empire, or how they let their consciences be eclipsed by what they consider duty or patriotism. Above all, I'll never understand why they are willing to take lives on someone else's say-so. What were the Nuremberg Trials about, anyway, but the primacy of individual conscience? What is all true theology about, after all, but the very same thing? Yet, as Thoreau noted in *Walden,* in nature the red ants incessantly fight the black ants, and probably always will.

Still, it doesn't surprise me that the most affecting message of commiseration I got about Miss Dutchie came from my novelist client and friend Rick Cooke, a retired XO on nuclear attack submarines.

Dear Ed,

We're so sorry to hear about Dutchess. I know you and Lynn showered her with love and affection all of her life and that she must have been one of the happiest dogs. From all the stories you told me about her, I know she was very special. Now she's running on young legs across endless green fields somewhere, finding a bone in every burrow. Please know that you and Lynn are in our prayers.

Aftermath

There are only
so many people
that you
can talk to,
and they aren't
here.
It took you years
to uncover them
and then they disappear.
And then you disappear.
  —Sidney Goldfarb,
  "To Make Them Monumental"

Sadie arrived on May Day, 2008. At slightly before eleven that Thursday morning a dark green Saab station wagon pulled into our driveway. Lynn had got me up an hour earlier, even though we had arrived fairly late the night before. I had taken Lynn the previous afternoon to a very good production of our favorite comedy in English, *The Importance of Being Earnest,* put on by the Pearl Theatre Company in the East Village. Afterward we had gone to dinner on the Upper East Side and then hurried home, packed, and left for the country. We had to be in place in the morning because Lynn had arranged for a woman from Homeward Bound to bring a Lab mix puppy to our house for me to meet. Lynn had seen the puppy the previous Saturday at Homeward Bound's weekly showing of rescue dogs in the parking lot of Benson's, the big pet store on Wolf Road in Albany. Lynn had liked the puppy but had been unable to make up her mind what we should do.

Lynn had heard the car pull in and had gone out into the yard. I put down the newspaper and my cup of coffee in the living room, walked to the back of the house and stepped out on the deck. There on the lawn to my left stood Lynn and the woman from Homeward Bound. Lynn introduced us. Her name was Lex. I immediately made the connection to the Latin word for "law." She had a very pleasant smile and held, crooked in her right arm, cradled against her chest, a black puppy wearing a calico kerchief around her neck printed in red and dotted with a flower pattern in blue. I immediately thought of Dale Evans on the old *Roy Rogers Show* and of Penny on the old

Sky King show aired on Saturday mornings when I was a kid.

Lynn said, "Why don't you hold her, honey?"

Lex stepped forward and we made a smooth transfer.

I noticed instantly that the puppy burrowed herself against my chest, head tucked in. She also had a slight tremble. It was a warm spring morning, so she wasn't cold. I stroked her and pulled her tighter against me. I also cupped both arms around her and rocked her slightly. I could feel her hiccupping nervously from time to time, in addition to the tremble, and I knew instantly that she'd been traumatized and it ticked me off. Lynn had mentioned that when she'd first met this puppy the previous Saturday she had seemed very depressed, even though children gravitated to her in Benson's parking lot and she seemed to respond well to them, if only in a subdued manner.

Lex said, "Her name's Azalea."

I thought, *How awkward.* And: *What a jawbreaker. Imagine repeating four syllables every time you wanted to call her.* But I said nothing.

Lynn suggested we go in the house and talk. She had lots of questions for Lex. In truth we were both wary of adopting a rescue dog because we'd heard horror stories of people getting the dogs when they were too old, or too traumatized, and then being unable to break them of bad, destructive, or even dangerous habits. I had my twenty nieces and nephews to consider when it came to any dog, and any dog Lynn and I owned needed to be completely compatible with children, especially since now two of my nieces had supplied me with a grandnephew and two grandnieces, all three toddlers, and another nephew had a third grandniece on the way.

In the house Lynn and Lex went into the dining room where Lex could explain matters to Lynn. Also, part of Homeward Bound's very responsible and admirable policy requires a home inspection visit prior to adoption of one of their rescue dogs by anyone. Lex had taken in our yard at a glance, and our house is fairly small, so she already had a full idea of what we could offer. The house sits on .78 of an acre. I remember that exactly from the closing twenty-one years ago. That means the yard is plenty big for a dog.

While Lynn and Lex talked I went into the living room and flopped into my armchair with Azalea. I had my coffee right next to me on the washstand but I didn't drink much of it. I was more fascinated with how upset this little puppy was. Clearly I could see Lynn's point about the depression but what worried me more was Azalea's obvious and acute anxiety. Of course I kept thinking of Dutchie at seven weeks and the unholy racket she had set up in the house right from the get-go, but this was somehow different and even more disturbing. I was stroking Azalea and trying to comfort her, but her hiccups grew more intense. They racked her whole rib cage. She shook violently each time she had one. I kept stroking her and started to talk to her. I was also talking in my head to Miss Dutchie, wondering what the hell we should do.

Before I knew it I was whispering to Azalea and stroking her and telling her things were not so bad. I told her I didn't like the fact that she was this upset. I kept thinking of how Dutchie would sometimes be so jealous if I showered too much affection on Pete Fenn or Caspar Fenn or Rosie Fenn or any other dog. Yet I knew bighearted Miss Dutchie would not be immune to this little puppy's ontological angst. As I held Azalea and stroked her and started to coo instead of talk to her, she started to come out of her fetal crouch against my chest and to climb up it with sharp little nails. They felt like tiny pitons. These she eventually wrapped around my neck and tried to cling ever tighter to me. Finally after much cooing and stroking the hiccupping subsided slightly and I told her softly, "Everything is going to be all right. I think you're Uncle Eddie's new girlfriend."

By now Lynn and Lex had talked for about an hour. I knew all the downside aspects of adopting a rescue dog. I considered them all now, once again, sitting in the sunshine in the living room. I knew that not even the dog people at

Homeward Bound knew what the "mix" was in this Lab mix misnamed Azalea. Lynn had met Azalea's littermate and the littermate had been brindled. This I figured meant probably boxer, greyhound, or pit bull. It was the pit bull that worried me when I thought of all the children in my extended family but I am nothing in life if not decisive. I got up with Azalea still clinging to me and went and stood in the doorway to the dining room, listening to the tail end of Lex's recitation of the instructions and obligations incumbent upon adopters of dogs from Homeward Bound. None of it daunted me.

"You just sign here," Lex said to Lynn, holding out the one-page contract.

Lynn hesitated and said, "But can't we just keep her for a trial weekend?"

"No," Lex said. "If you take her she's yours. Otherwise we'll put her back in the adoption pool and show her again Saturday."

Leaning against the doorjamb I thought, like a good AA, which I'm not, *Should I say the Serenity Prayer to help with this decision?* Half the time it annoys me. I heard my father say with his unmatched courage, "Nothing ventured, nothing gained. The Lord hates a coward." With the puppy's heart beating against my right hand I flashed back on Dutchie's heart beating against it on June 9, 2006, three minutes before it stopped forever. Could I make it through that trauma again? I heard my mother say, "Grow up. Life is just one damn thing after another." My mother was to Yeats's indomitable Irishry what the meter in Paris is to all measurement in the metric system. She had undergone extreme unction twice, in labor with each of my last two siblings, and both times she was supposed to bleed to death from hemorrhages. Instead she survived, just as she survived diabetes, breast cancer, a heart "event," and a series of minor strokes; survived, that is, until she died in the same room she was born in, in her eighty-seventh year, eight months after Sadie arrived, less than two weeks before Christmas 2008. Shortly before that, when I had phoned her exasperated with Sadie, she had told me, "Be patient with her."

As it turned out, my mom was right. When Lynn needed a second lumpectomy this spring, on April Fool's Day, of all bad omens, Sadie was a great comfort to both of us. The omen was wrong and we again got off easy. The lump was benign.

Still leaning against the doorjamb that fateful May Day, I remembered thinking: *You're projecting again, idiot, maybe this puppy will outlive you.* Finally, to cap this decision, I channeled Gerard, who loved what he called the short version of the Serenity Prayer, which I loved too and which he never failed to invoke: "Fuck it."

I heard myself say, "Just sign it, Lynn."

. . .

She was ours. Lex had assured us we could change her name. Lynn called her Sadie. A week later we took her to Philadelphia and my mother christened her "Sadie, the Shady Lady." I went to work on her that first weekend in Coxsackie, before our trip to Philly, but got nowhere fast. She clung, she cowered, she clawed her way into my flesh, trying always to hold me tighter, but most of all she moped. All day that Thursday in our excitement Lynn and I were hyperactive. Lynn went into the attic and pulled out all of Dutchie's toys and dog beds and the car bed and everything. I drove to Walmart and bought her a new bed to put in the crate Ruth Leonard brought over for us to use in the country. Excitement ran high. But Sadie still brooded and moped.

I worked on her to no avail. All day Friday she was clinging and seemingly comatose. Then on Saturday I felt the exhilaration I always feel on the first Saturday in May, Derby Day. With Thanksgiving and the Fourth of July, for me Derby Day completes the trinity of great American holidays. In the afternoon Lynn went out to do some shopping and run some errands. I was left alone with Sadie. I don't know how it happened. But it happened.

I was cooing and cuddling with her while seated in the armchair in the living room when suddenly she got rambunctious in my arms. I immediately set her down on the rug. Then I faux hollered, "Come back here," as she stared up at me. I pretended to struggle to get out of the chair. She lit out for the dining room. I tromped my feet hard in feigned pursuit of her. She scampered out into the dining room and circled the table, me trailing her, stomping hard, making false threats.

She went ballistic. I had to chase her and catch her and toss her on her back and rub her down and let her nip at my hands and arms for almost an hour. She was tearing in and out of rooms on the first floor and rocketing off the dog beds and furniture. I had never seen a puppy that happy. She tried to vault onto the sofa, smacked into the cushions, tumbled over backward onto the rug, and sprang back onto her feet and bolted for the dining room again. I was laughing so hard I could hardly chase her, and twice I had to sit down and catch my breath.

Then we heard the back door open into the kitchen and Lynn came in. Sadie continued to tear around the first floor. I heard Lynn walking down the short hallway to the living room. She entered just as Sadie shot past her and tripped on her own big round L.L. Bean dog bed in front of the sofa and somersaulted onto the bed and then straight off it, landing hard on the pine floor on the other side of it.

"What have you done to her? She'll hurt herself," Lynn said.

I was laughing too hard to answer. I knew she was going to be just fine.

That afternoon I thrilled to the strains of "My Old Kentucky Home" and loved watching Big Brown win the Derby. Sadie was curled up on her big round fluffy L.L. Bean bed in front of the sofa, where Lynn perched. I was stationed in my armchair, eyes riveted on the TV screen. The race went off beautifully. Then it happened. That big beautiful filly named Eight Belles that finished second tumbled to the turf and I said to Lynn, "Oh, no, she'll have to be euthanized." I was flashing back on Ruffian being euthanized in the summer of 1975 after her match race at Belmont. With Eight Belles it was Barbaro all over again, but without the suspense of the half-year struggle to survive. It was over in an instant. The track vet euthanized Eight Belles right on the turf.

I immediately thought of Dutchie's ashes still in the tan canister with the blue flowers on it tucked away in the bottom drawer of the sideboard in the dining room. Maybe we'll never get to them, to distribute them at the river, as we planned. We kept putting it off, forgetting about it, denying it. Somehow it was too final, not to have something of Dutchie in the house. I thought of just how much you can love an animal. I remembered reading a while back in the *New York Sun* an article about a woman who bit a pit bull when the pit bull attacked her dog. She had loved her dog that much. That had made me feel better about my own murderous outburst when a pit bull attacked Miss Dutchie in the Museum of Natural History dog run years ago. I had kicked the pit bull off Miss Dutchie and then, when threatened with violence by its sadistic owner, backed him totally down, physically and verbally, though he was a head taller and at least thirty pounds heavier than me. The whole episode had depressed me though. But maybe I wasn't so crazy after all, being homicidally deranged in defense of my dog.

Loving Sadie up to the point where she shook off her depression had its downside though. I didn't know she would become so animated and happy over the next six months that Lynn and I would have to take steps to calm her so she didn't wreck the house. She had a habit of wilding when excited that could get out of hand. Lynn and I speculated that the "mix" in Lab mix was House Breaker, though we knew no such breed existed. Sadie was dangerous around shoes and clothes and furniture. She had eviscerated my favorite slippers; that got her in bad odor with me for an entire hour. I also had no clue that she didn't care for the law of inertia and thought it was a good idea for the two of us to occupy the same space at the same time. She would wedge herself between the back of my chair and me and cant her head around my shoulder. She did it to Lynn too. We sat on the edge of the chair like Rodin's *Thinker,* watching TV or reading, all the while trying gently to break her of this habit but not succeeding.

I also didn't know that she would become such a raucous barker that she would startle us awake in the middle of the night whenever she heard an animal move outside in the yard in the country, or even whenever she heard footsteps outside in the corridor in our apartment in the city. I didn't know as well that in her ecstasy she would sometimes become annoyingly unruly, even toppling me over at the curb one day on Columbus Avenue, spraining my ankle and forcing me, panicked, to run hobbling into oncoming traffic, snatch her up to a symphony of screeching brakes, and then somehow sprint with her on my aching ankle to the other side of the street.

Yet she was so happy and so demonstrative about everything that it was infectious and exhilarating to be around. A few weeks back we brought her to the country after a long spell in the city and she became so animated when Chris Warren arrived in the yard with Alice and Jasmine that Sadie spun like a top on her butt like a break-dancer. She is so athletic she's like a Chinese gymnast, using the furniture as her parallel bars and horse; and she runs with me, just the way Suzie did and unlike Dutchie, and with stamina that is off the charts. I do three or four miles, she does eight or ten, quartering the fields, exploring the woods, running ahead, treeing squirrels more avidly than Dutchie and yelping and baying at them and leaping against the trunks of the trees like a coon hound. Indoors, she also doesn't care how many computers are on, unlike Miss Dutchie. She likes to sit in the room with you the whole time Lynn and I work at our keyboards, being, in Bill Contardi's memorable words, a "great companion."

At the time I told Lynn to sign the adoption papers I didn't know that "Azalea" had been rescued from a "kill shelter." Wrap your mind around that oxymoron and tell me that it doesn't in general say a lot about life on this planet a great deal of the time, especially in corporations. So I was right in my initial instinct that she had been traumatized. I later learned that she had been abandoned in a mineshaft in Alabama along with her thirteen littermates. It was near a highway. Nine of the puppies perished, run over by vehicles; four survived, including "Azalea," aka "Sadie, the Shady Lady." I did know that besides running with her, I liked to ride to meetings in the country with her perched on the passenger seat of my new Camry as I blasted Eddy Arnold's "The Cattle Call" from the CD, a song about as American as the yen for the open road. I did know too that when she vexed me with her out-of-control behavior she had been sent by the fates or the gods to shed some light on my father's and my mother's cross to bear in dealing with me, a reprobate and a rapscallion coming on the heels of my placid and self-contained older brother. Compared to Miss Dutchie's regal princess Sadie was a hellacious rascal.

I knew when Eight Belles went down that I would always cherish Luis Buñuel's great line, "I'm still an atheist, thank God."

But I also knew that it would always give me pause to recall the great line I heard the Monday night after Sadie arrived when I attended the upstate Norton Hill meeting, two days after Eight Belles had died. A young woman I admire immensely choked out through tears and a cracking voice, because she had got her two daughters back in family court, that her God was "a God of Restoration."

I think of that every time Sadie lines up opposite me at my computer or in my armchair and goes into a low-grade growl and slaps a paw on my knee. When I stare down at her in feigned anger, I always receive in return a sneering grin. It's the same grin the incomparable Miss Dutchie used to flash at me. It's the grin that actualized the admonition my psychiatrist gave me for years. Whenever I defended my grinding workaholism to him, I'd say, "It's what Freud said. The meaning of life is love and work."

"And play," he'd always add.

The Sadie grin says what the Dutchie grin always did, just the one thing to me: "Game on."